True Stories of the

X-Amish

is
published by

Neu Leben, Inc.
(New Life)

Questions or Comments
write to:

Neu Leben, Inc.
P.O. Box 179
Horse Cave, Ky.
42749-0179

ii

True Stories of the
X-Amish

as told to
Ottie A. Garrett
Writer and Editor

Interviews and Revisions
by
R. Irene Garrett
O.A. Garrett

Editing by
Tonya Parsons Cesler

Photographs

Cover photo by: Mike Bogue
Cover design by: Ottie A. Garrett
Inside photos by: Ottie A. Garrett

Interview Recording
Audio/video operator: Monte S. Garrett

Artist
Ben N. Garrett

Editor's Note

The stories you are about to read are true, although certain names and places have been changed in order to protect the identities of certain individuals who wish to remain anonymous. Neu Leben, Inc. has taken every precaution to assure that all the stories contained in this book are as factual as humanly possible.

This book and Neu Leben, Inc. by no means is trying to portray the Old Order Amish as a corrupt group of religious people, as in all societies there are good and bad. We here at Neu Leben, Inc. are showing a side that is hidden by the leaders of the Old Order Amish communities. Neu Leben, Inc. is giving those who left the Old Order Amish an opportunity to tell their side of the story.

The individuals described throughout this book are all from the Old Order Amish. Therefore to make things simpler we will just use the word Amish.

Acknowledgement

Finding the words to express my gratitude to all the people who in one form or another have helped to make this book a reality has proved to be most difficult, to say the least. For mere words seem so little a gesture to make to such fine people.

First the X-Amish, Ltd. without all of your help, I'd still be planning and dreaming. To the writing staff, Meredith Johnston, Jennifer Hardy, Michelle Coleman, Sue Neagle, Tonya Cesler, Marilyn Greer, Daniel Curry and Jennifer Wade, you have handled with care and dignity each and every chapter in this book. I wish each of you much success in the future. To Lonnie Douglas and Connie Beech of Gerald Printing, for their ability to turn a manuscript into a book; to Tonya P. Cesler for her editing skills and her expertise with the English language; to Jennifer Hardy and Marilyn Greer for their typing skills; to my technical and computer advisors, Ben Garrett and Faye Talbott; to my five children, Chad, Monte, Joshua, Matthew, and my little girl Samantha; also to my father, Ottie Sr. and his wife Pat, my love and best wishes always; to my wife Irene, it's been a long time in coming; and finally to the ones who shared their lives and stories that are told in this book, you are the book, to all of you, my humble,

Thank you,

Dedication

This book is dedicated in two parts; first, to my X-Amish wife, Irene who has had to endure so much heartache and yet has given so much love to those of us around her; and second, to the memory of my son Phillip, and my mother Ersie Jewell, never to be forgotten in hearts and minds.

Introduction

There is one word which serves as the linchpin, connecting all of these stories of the X-Amish, one word which weaves through each account as a thematic backdrop. The word is freedom. Freedom to choose where to live and how to live, freedom to choose what to believe and what to reject. Freedom to make the basic decisions of life.

While most of us take such freedom for granted, the stories that follow describe people who longed for yet lived without the fundamental right to choose the course of their living. The struggle to break away, to be set free are what makes the subject matter of this book so compelling. In each chapter we meet a new character of set of characters, a different set of circumstances and a different set of reasons or motivations but always the backdrop remains the same- the desire to be free.

As you read please take note of this common theme. I believe it offers insight and some measure for explanation for why these people, Ed and Levi and the Yoders and the rest, risked so much and gave up so much of the familiar and safe in their lives. Like I said before, the subject is compelling. If you are like me, by the end of the book, a sense of profound gratitude will have grown up, gratitude for what we often overlook- the gift of freedom.

Rev. J.A. Bettermann
6/18/98

Foreword

Looking back in history we find the beginning of the Amish faith in Western Europe. It was all started by a group of people in 1525 who refused to allow their children to be baptized by the Catholic Church. They felt that children did not understand salvation; children could not understand Christ's call of discipleship. Because of this belief, they became known as Anabaptists. The Catholic Church felt that these Anabaptists were rejecting the authority of the church; therefore, members of this renegade group were imprisoned and threatened. Finally, thousands of Anabaptists were killed because they refused to give in to the pressure placed on them by the local authorities and the Catholic Church.

Most Anabaptist groups were quiet and peaceful and wanted only to be left alone, but there were other groups of Anabaptists who took up the sword. In 1534, they decided to create an Anabaptist state. This time the Anabaptists did the persecuting and punishing of those that would not bend to their beliefs. By 1535, the Catholic Church and the Protestants destroyed the aggressive Anabaptists in a battle in Münster. Because of these warring Anabaptists, the Catholic Church now considered all Anabaptists to be violent and militant revolutionaries and punishment would be swift and final.

The Anabaptist movement became unorganized, and they needed a leader. A Catholic priest by the name of Menno Simons had been watching and learning of the Anabaptist movement for some time. Menno had become a priest in 1524- the same time that Martin Luther was making sweeping changes in Western European Catholic beliefs. During this time Menno began to question his own beliefs and those of the Catholic Church around 1532. Finally, Simons broke from the Catholic Church and joined the Anabaptist movement. When this happened, the church put a price on his head.

Menno Simons could read, write, and be added organization to the then unorganized groups of Anabaptists throughout Western Europe. It was around the year 1536 Menno Simons became the leader of the Anabaptist movement, and soon after that his followers were called Mennonite Anabaptists.

After more than 150 years of struggle and controversy was it possible that unity was on the horizon for the Mennonite Anabaptist movement? In the year 1690, an elder of the Alsatian Anabaptist Mennonites began some rather innovative religious practices. This caused some unrest among the other Mennonite groups in Switzerland and Germany. Hans Reist, a Mennonite elder and leader of the largest group of Swiss Mennonites, reprimanded this unorthodox Mennonite leader named Jacob Ammann. Reist and Ammann soon became rivals. In 1693, Ammann, in a confrontation with Reist followers, excommunicated Reist and his leaders, causing shock waves throughout the Mennonite communities in Western Europe. Jacob Ammann was causing a schism, or a division within the Mennonite church. When leaders of other Mennonite areas tried to get Jacob Ammann to listen to reason, he would in turn excommunicate them and anyone who disagreed with him. There would be no reconciliation or truce.

Jacob Ammann wrote letters to other Mennonite groups in his quest to change the doctrine of the Mennonite church. Some of Ammann's ideas on new doctrine were that men would wear their beards untrimmed, the use of hook and eyes to fasten coats, foot washing, two communion services a year instead of once a year, stricter rules on the ban, shunning, and excommunicating members. Ammann believed that there was no gray area only right or wrong. Ammann felt that humility and simplicity was the way.

After years of banning and excommunicating nearly half of all Mennonites, calmer heads began to reason with Jacob Ammann. After much soul searching and consideration of the consequences he had caused the Mennonite church, Jacob Ammann and some of his leaders decided to try and rejoin the main stream Mennonite church. In order to show repentance, Jacob Ammann excommunicated himself and his leaders. The Reist group refused but were pleased that Ammann and his leaders admitted they were wrong. In 1699, and again in 1700, Ammann tried to rejoin the Mennonites, but the

Mennonites felt it was too late because there would always be indifference and separation by doctrine and interpretation of scripture and tradition. Jacob Ammann had excommunicated over half of the Mennonites; the Mennonites excommunicated Jacob Ammann, and finally Jacob Ammann excommunicated himself from his own group.

Jacob Ammann, spiritual leader and founder of the Amish faith, died while he was still banned and excommunicated. Today the Amish still ban, shun, and excommunicate any member who differs or leaves the church.

In the years before his death and after, Amish groups began leaving Europe for the New World. By 1830, there were no Amish left in Europe, for all had come to America. Settling first in Pennsylvania in 1720, they then moved west as our country grew.

* * *

It's Saturday morning in early summer. The sun is shining; the sky is clear, and the temperature is a comfortable 78 degrees. What a beautiful day to take the family on a drive to the country.

You are pointing out local attractions to your children, when you notice an unusual road sign. It's a yellow warning sign with a horse and buggy, which means there might be Amish in this area.

As you continue your drive, you begin to notice farms with wind mills turning in the wind. Rounding a curve, there you see it, a real horse and buggy with real Amish people. As you pass the buggy your kids are really getting excited now. They've never seen anything like this except in Social Studies books at school or pictures in different types of magazines.

Up ahead you notice you're coming to a cross road and wouldn't you know it, there under a big poplar tree is a vegetable stand consisting of a couple hand made tables. Tied to the tree are two horses unhitched from the buggy. The stand is loaded with all types of homegrown vegetables, yellow sweet corn, green beans, bright red vine ripened tomatoes, radishes, and crisp leaf lettuce. On another table there are freshly baked goodies that make your mouth water from the aroma of it all. Homemade breads, 40 or 50 packages of noodles, and sweet cinnamon rolls with caramel frosting. Dozens of cookies, raisin oatmeal, peanut butter, molasses, and sugar cookies.

Pies, oh my,all kinds, strawberry, blackberry, peach, apple, and rhubarb pies.

Your children run over to the horses tied to the tree and you warn them to stay away. You tell them they may look at them, but do not try to touch, and stay away from behind the horses because they may kick if they are startled.

You begin to closely examine the vegetables and other goodies before you. You ask the Amish woman the price of the corn, and she responds in broken English with a definite accent, maybe German. You notice her hands as she picks up a bundle of six ears of corn. Her hands are chapped and callused, with dirt under her fingernails, but she is a farmer's wife. Maybe she had to pick most of these vegetables before setting up her stand.

As you walk around the tables, you can't help but notice the man with her who is putting more food on the table. He is probably her husband. You notice his shaggy beard; it is about six inches long with streaks of gray, and he has no mustache. You wonder why but you don't ask because he doesn't seem too friendly. Besides he won't look you in the eyes; he seems to avoid looking at you or anyone at all for that matter. There are other cars pulling into this vegetable stand and now more people are asking, how much? As you continue to look around, you spot young Amish children about the same age as your two children, the little boy about 8 or 9 and the little girl about 5 or 6. You see that the little boy is taking care of his sister. Their clothes all look as if they're home made, only buttons, no zippers. The woman's dress has straight pins and no buttons, even though the temperature is about 80 degrees now. Their clothes have to be hot because of such dark colors, plus the little boy and his father are wearing hats. The little girl and her mother are both wearing heavy black bonnets. Your children come running up to you wearing shorts and short sleeve shirts with fancy tennis shoes with some famous person's name all over them. Both of the Amish children are bare foot. Finally the question pops into your mind, I wonder what it would be like to be and live like the Amish? That would be a very normal question to ask. You're only human, but guess what, so are the Amish. It makes me wonder do the Amish or at least some of the Amish ever ask themselves, What would it be like to be English? (English is what the Amish call everyone who is not Amish.)

Today there are over 230 Amish communities in 22 states, mostly in the mid-West. Amish are found in rural areas because the majority of Amish are farmers. According to the last estimate there are approximately 140,000 Old Order Amish in this country. That means the Amish are less than one half of one percent of the total population in this country.

There is no central leadership among the Amish. There are over 1,100 church groups, and in each of these church groups, which consist of 22 to 28 families, there is one Bishop who is the undisputed spiritual leader.

Each group also has two or three ministers and one deacon, all of whom have obtained their position by a lot system. The Amish believe this lot system is as if you are chosen by God. The Amish faith is classified as a Christian group that claim to be conscientious objectors, and they are recognized by the United States Government as being just that. Most Amish groups across America abstain from owning telephones, cars, tractors, or even having running water or indoor plumbing in their homes. Please note that I said abstain from owning. Even though they don't own, they don't mind using a phone or hiring a driver with a van, pickup or car to take them wherever they want to go.

Amish believe in God's word which says to multiply; most have very large families. Amish families average 8 to 10 children per family. This way the Amish children can work around the farm and all do just as soon as they are old enough to get out there and work. A large family ensures that all of the chores that go with the farm will be taken care of.

The stories you are about to read deal with Old Order Amish families in rural America. It has been estimated that for every 5 children in the Amish, one will leave the Amish faith to go to the outside world, as the Amish put it. The reason for leaving will differ in each case, some because they want a better life, others because of abuse, and others for religious freedoms. When these Amish people make their decision to leave, they not only leave the Amish, they will also leave behind their families, mother, father, brothers and sisters— everyone, because the Amish will place them in what is called the ban. This means that the Amish no longer recognize them as being one of them. Now considered an outsider, they will be shunned, meaning no

Amish person can take anything from them, eat with them, or have any other type of communications, unless of course they are trying to come back to the Amish.

The people in these stories don't want to go back to the Old Order Amish ways. They only want to tell their stories and live their lives as they choose. Oh sure, they would love to see their families but not on the terms the Amish leaders have set forth. I lived near the Amish for more than 10 years, I knew several families, and became close friends with some of them. It was several years before I ever heard the term X-Amish. I had no idea anyone ever left, but like so many things in life, nothing is perfect even though it may appear that way on the outside. None of the stories are made up or fiction. Each story is true. As you read their stories try and understand their need to explain the reason they left the Amish.

Table of Contents

Editor's Note V

Acknowledgment VII

Dedication IX

Introduction by Rev. Jim Bettermann XI

Foreword by Ottie A. Garrett.......................XIII

Contents XIX

Chapter 1- LeRoy 1
writer: Meredith Johnston

Chapter 2- Dan..11
writers: Jennifer Hardy & Michelle Coleman

Chapter 3- Joni...21
writer: Meredith Johnston

Chapter 4- Ed..35
writer: Sue Neagle

Chapter 5- Mannie & Johnny 49
writer: Tonya Parsons Cesler

Chapter 6- Mattie...55
writer: Marilyn Greer

Chapter 7- George & Lydia 73
writer: Jennifer Hardy

Chapter 8- Joe & Rachel 83
writer: Jennifer Hardy

Chapter 9- Levi & Miriam..............................97
writer: Daniel Curry

Chapter 10- The Yoders 105
writer: Jennifer Wade

Open Letter From Eli.....................................117

Conclusion by Ottie A. Garrett...................119

Man who hold bird in hand say bird is his. If he let bird go and bird come back, bird really his. If bird not come back, bird never was his.

—Old Chinese Proverb

Chapter One
LeRoy

It was almost completely dark. Only the soft light of the moon peeked in through the small window of LeRoy's basement room. As the night hours closed in on morning, LeRoy hurriedly pulled on his clothes, all the while trying desperately not to wake his other brothers who slept soundly all around him. If any one were to wake and discover him, all the time and effort that had gone into the planning would be wasted.

For two months, through only a few letters to his brother, LeRoy had planned his escape from a life he felt had him locked in chains. The plan was to have his brother pick him up at the school-house at midnight, and they would leave from there. LeRoy was to work for his uncle Andy in construction and live with his brother. He would begin to experience the life of tee-shirts, blue jeans, and rock-and-roll, and he was ready.

Slowly he opened the basement door that led to his new life and was slapped with the cold hard air. Holding back his excitement, he closed the door softly into place and started across the field. From where he was standing at the house, he could see the school. He wanted to run full force to his destination, but he knew he had to play it smart or risk being caught.

Despite the chill of the air, the winter thaw had already begun to show its effects all around the farm. The trees were beginning to show the first signs of rebirth brought on by warm middays. The ground was soft under LeRoy's feet as he moved carefully across the field.

His heart pounded louder and louder as he got closer to the

school. Every few steps he turned cautiously to make sure he was not being followed by an angry father. Slowly but surely he made it to the schoolhouse and slipped quietly into the woodshed located directly behind it.

He found a spot in the corner where he was sure to see any approaching cars and began his watch. The warmth of the shed surrounded LeRoy like the old quilt on his bed, the one that he would have been wrapped snugly in at that very moment on any normal night. It did not take long for his eyes to grow heavy and for the adrenaline that was coursing through him to dissipate. Before he knew it, he was drifting off into a sweet but guarded sleep.

The blackness became lighter and lighter as visions of the farm unfolded beneath his closed lids, and he remembered a day not that long ago. It was the day that had sparked his fire to explore a world he had never known. It was a day that he would remember vividly throughout his entire life.

LeRoy was only thirteen years old, and it was his first winter away from school and the farm. The day started out as usual. He came downstairs with his other seven brothers and his sister, all making their way to the feast that was laid out for breakfast.

The long wooden table held numerous bowls and plates, some brimming to the top with red and black berries, hot cereal, sausage links, and steamed bread; others waiting patiently at the side for someone to fill their emptiness. The sizzle of eggs on the hot cast iron skillet ceased as they all gathered around the table and found their seats. Mom rationed out the eggs; everyone ate their eggs over easy with just a bit of salt.

With bellies full, the family made their way out into the fields to begin the daily chores. First, the obligatory milking of the cows, with everyone doing their share, and then feeding. The animals, locked in the barn during the night, were let out in the morning to get their exercise.

The sun streamed down upon the long rows of corn, sparkling upon the dew that still clung to them. The tall shocks stood like soldiers as the men hitched up the two wagons. A long heavy chain was hooked to one side at the back of each wagon, then pulled tighter for better effect. The two wagons made their way through the field letting the chains knock the shocks down to dry.

This went on until lunch time and even after. Finally, the dried corn shocks were loaded up to take to the shredders. The corn would be made into feed and meal and the stalks into bedding for the horses.

LeRoy was given lead of one of the wagons. He jumped into the seat and pulled out into the path. Maybe LeRoy was caught up in enjoying the beauty of the day. Maybe weariness had already set in, and he closed his eyes for just a minute too long. Or maybe he just was not paying attention because on the next curve, he did not make it around as smoothly as he should have.

He pulled the reins hard, but somehow the wagon just did not make it past the obstacle of the fence row. He barely nudged up against an old rotten post, and it fell to the ground. Accidents happen to the best of us, but in Amish country, they don't just slip by.

LeRoy turned to see the angry look that had already plastered itself across the face of his father. LeRoy was forewarned about the punishment that would be dealt to him for making such a foolish mistake. First, though, he was to finish his chores.

An eternity would pass in the time that LeRoy had to complete his chores. Sweat beaded across his brow and even the cool breeze of winter could not knock it away. Would he have to pick a switch and take a beating in front of his brothers and sister? Would he have to go to bed without supper? Or, as all children hope, was the punishment simply waiting to be punished? Of course not, it never was.

After letting the cows in for the day and doing the nightly feeding, the verdict was handed down: his punishment...the strap. He should have seen it coming. Determined not to give his father any indication that he was hurting him, LeRoy tried to take it like a man. If only he had not been so angry, he never would have cried.

It was that night that LeRoy made the announcement to his brothers that he was going to leave the Amish as soon as he got old enough. It was immediately brought to his attention that he would go to hell, but LeRoy was past the point of caring. If he was going to go to hell, he was at least going to do it his way.

The images of the farm drifted back into memory as LeRoy blinked himself back into consciousness. It had started raining, and a thick fog lay over the land. LeRoy hoped that his brother had not

3

decided to turn around in the bad weather, and if he was on the road, that he was safe. As the morning hours closed in on three a.m., LeRoy's ride to freedom pulled into the drive.

LeRoy started his new adventure of the English lifestyle by going to the city to visit some of his brother's friends. They ended up at his brother's house by two p.m. the following day and had to rest; they were going to a concert that night.

Thousands of people filed into the arena. English girls in short skirts and English boys in cowboy hats surrounded LeRoy on all sides. Hot pink neon lights advertised beer and nachos. Laughter and high pitched squeals of excitement filled the smoky air. LeRoy's heart started beating a little faster, and he could not help but be swayed by the intensity that gripped the room. In the blink of an eye, all the people found their feet and cheered as Alan Jackson made his way out onto the stage.

He did not know the songs, but LeRoy clapped in rhythm with the audience. A smile spread uncontrollably across his face. He wished the night would never end, but eventually he fell exhausted into his new bed.

Months passed swiftly with each day bringing a new adventure. LeRoy found the job he was doing for his uncle to be routine, but fulfilling. He could at least thank the Amish for teaching him the importance of hard work and the skills to do it.

Late one evening as LeRoy had just undressed for bed, there came a hard knock on the door. Reluctantly, he pulled his blue jeans back on and went to answer the door bare chested. As he pulled the door open, his heart flew up to his throat. Beyond the safety of the heavy wood was the event that he had hoped to avoid. A van load had come into town to take LeRoy home.

LeRoy stood there feeling like an untagged puppy staring down the local dog catcher. Were they going to throw a rope around his neck and drag him unwillingly into that looming dark vehicle parked in the driveway? He looked around speechless for help, and was happy to see his brother rounding the corner.

David, LeRoy's brother, invited the crowd of people in, and they made their way into the living room. With a firm hand, he grabbed LeRoy's shoulder and gave him a look that said, "Don't worry," "I'll handle this," all at the same time. LeRoy nodded at the unspoken

4

promise and followed his brother to join the others.

LeRoy knew most of the people who stood there, not asking, but threatening to take him home. There were aunts, uncles, cousins, and a few others surrounding the two men. His father and mother did not come because LeRoy had explained to them that he would come home if and when he was ready. It was mainly people who thought that LeRoy needed to go back to the Amish, and as far as LeRoy was concerned, it was not any of their business.

David did most of the talking, and LeRoy did most of the listening. It was everything that he expected and nothing that he had not heard before. LeRoy was doomed to hell, but could easily be saved by going back to his religion.

Religion, LeRoy thought. Amish was not a religion, rather it was a way of life held together by man-made rules that no one could question without being damned. Everyone had traditions, but the Amish turn theirs into a lifestyle.

Voices raised and biblical quotes spewed forth, each for the user's own purpose. LeRoy stood with false strength behind his brother, wishing that they would just leave. Finally, they did and without LeRoy. Night had turned into morning as the van drove away, and LeRoy and his brother retired to their rooms.

Staring at the ceiling, LeRoy tried to quiet the voices that continued to ring through his head. The truth was, he did not know the truth. Fear crept into his body and he had to try to convince himself that what he was doing was right, or at least it was okay for the moment.

LeRoy had always thought that if he went out and participated in the real world, that he could go back to the Amish someday and be saved if need be. Then opportunities that he had never dreamed of opened right before his eyes. Things that LeRoy had never considered possible were within his reach, and he was not ready to pull his hand back just yet. Maybe he never would be.

Every night as he lay in bed reading, he thought about the possibility of furthering his education. It would be a dream come true to finish high school, and then maybe a college education. LeRoy thought that education was one of the most important things available to English people, for it was something to cherish and never get enough of. He wanted to be full of information, to read and learn of different people and places. He wanted to soak in everything and then reach for more. As the thoughts of all the wonderful things that were now possible for him filled his head, the voices died into silence and his lids slid closed.

Time once again flew by, measured not in months this time but in years. LeRoy had little contact with the Amish and preferred life much better that way. It was not until the phone call saying that LeRoy's grandfather had passed on that he had to face them once more, this time, hopefully, on his own terms.

It was a sunny day and full of promise when LeRoy kissed Misty, the love of his life, goodbye and slid into the car to head back to the farm. Thoughts ran rampant through his mind as the trees blurred into one long green line and the fenceposts disappeared. He was driving faster than he normally would have, and he hoped that there were no cops around.

LeRoy did not take too kindly to police. He thought they were cocky. They were just more enforcers of man-made rules. LeRoy did believe that the English lifestyle gave people the right to live however they wished as long as they obeyed the laws. People, though, have their own opinions about what the law should be. He pushed the gas pedal down just a tad farther.

After a few hours, the road became more familiar and the distance that led from his present to his past grew shorter. LeRoy could count on his hands the number of times that he had taken that road since he had left the Amish. He did not get to see his family that often, and it was definitely a sore spot. His mother was the only one who kept up the correspondence, and this year, she missed his birthday.

The road that led to the farm was just ahead, and LeRoy pulled in slowly and parked along the side leaving his car at the end of the road. One of the times he had visited, his father had told him never to bring the car up there again. He did not want anyone seeing it, and he did not want the children to be influenced by the material goods of the English world.

He walked up to the house and was greeted by his mother who, despite the past, truly seemed to miss him. Soon after came his father silently holding out a pile of clothes that LeRoy was to put on. He had decided in the car that he would return to Amish clothes for the ceremony. It was one thing he could do to make the difficult day go a little easier.

He took the familiar-looking pile of clothes and went inside to put them on. It was the suit that had been made for him for his baptism into the church, a day that never came. The shirt was snug across the chest but not enough for anyone to notice. The jacket felt tight around his arms, and the trousers were just a bit too short for LeRoy's liking.

As he gazed in the mirror, he had to remind himself that the clothes did not mean anything, and they would come off much easier than they were put on. The thought passed through his mind that it was very symbolic that a suit that was made to celebrate life would be worn instead to a funeral. His life as an Amish man was truly over.

His grandfather was laid to rest with little ceremony, a simple burial for a simple man. LeRoy and David stayed isolated from the group and heard their names merely in passing whispers between the people. It was much that way all through the day, except for old friends who jokingly would ask when LeRoy was coming back.

The boys were not included in many conversations, but happened to overhear quite a few. The most interesting one was about one of the neighbor boys who had left the Amish and no one knew exactly where he was. Of course everyone had a theory, but nothing was definite.

There had been one time when LeRoy had helped one of his cousins leave the Amish. The boy said that he knew he would go back one day, and he did. The van never did come after him, rather someone just called one day and asked him to come home. He said he would if someone would come and get him, and they did.

It was sad, LeRoy thought. When they decide to leave the Amish, they need to tell their parents. If some are afraid that their parents will talk them into staying, then they should at least leave a note or make a phone call to let them know where they are.

LeRoy knew that most of the people who left did so because they were angry, and this boy would probably come straggling back in a few days. If you're going to leave, just leave, LeRoy thought. There is no sense in leaving if you know you are going to come back. Leave for the right reasons, too, not just because you're pissed off. Feeling irritated at the subject, LeRoy walked back towards the house alone.

The table was full of all the wonderful dishes that LeRoy could remember from his childhood. There was a large bowl full of fluffy mashed potatoes and beside them the gravy, green beans, corn, bread, meatballs, and sausage links. The table was filled with plates for the family, and two were set off to the side for LeRoy and his older brother.

The two boys were neither invited to the table, nor allowed to fill their own plates. A decent portion was given to each as they were once more isolated from the group, and the others were able to help themselves. LeRoy and David ate in a tense silence, which gave LeRoy more time to think.

As he looked at his family sitting around the dinner table, his throat became so tight that he could no longer swallow. He could not hear what they were saying because he was no longer listening, only watching. It was like watching a movie and only wishing that you could be part of the script.

He had missed the slow transformation of his sister and now saw the young lady instead of the girl he remembered. His father had gotten older, and LeRoy could not help wonder if he had been the cause of some of the wrinkles that lined his eyes. His mother would occasionally join the conversation, and her smile would peek through, but never lingered too long.

The conversation was lively with the boys getting a little loud and then being shushed back down. Despite the day's events, there was even some joy. The words did not matter though, only the picture. It was definitely the portrait of a family that LeRoy was no longer a part of. He had to admit to himself that this was what he missed the most.

He longed deep in his heart to be accepted by a family again, his family. He wanted to sit in on big meals and talk about the day's events, the weather, or nothing at all. He wanted to feel the love that he once felt when he lived there, but it was out of reach, so he pushed the feelings down.

He thought of one day having his own family, maybe one with Misty, and a house full of kids. He would teach them about their heritage, about where their father had come from, and how to accept people for who they were. He even wanted to review the German alphabet so he could teach his kids the language he grew up speaking.

He would have a house full. He would tell them to get an education and not only dream the impossible, but also achieve it. He would listen to them when they needed to talk and accept their mistakes with patience and kindness. Above all he would love them, no matter what they did.

For someone who was not under the ban, you sure could have fooled LeRoy. It was almost too much to bear. At the end of the long day, LeRoy pulled off the suit and thankfully dressed again in English clothes. They felt as good as the first stretch after a long night's sleep. Happy now at the image reflected in the mirror, LeRoy thumped himself in the chest and went to say his good-byes.

His mother gave him a tight hug and made soft promises to write soon. He gave his father a firm handshake, but no words passed between the two. There were waves at the door from his younger brothers and his sister as he headed back towards his car.

The wind in his hair was refreshing as he drove home. Home, that had a nice ring to it. It did not matter that it was not located on a farm with eight other people. It only mattered that there was someone there waiting for him, someone who loved him very much a job that was good and honest, and a whole world of opportunities.

Chapter Two

Dan

An anguished man releases himself from a secluded life of oppression to embrace an outside world of opportunity. That is the story of Dan Beachy. Leaving was not easy, but in order to live a happy life, Dan knew that he had to leave the only life he had ever known. What he left behind was abuse and intolerance, and what he was searching for in the outside world was a limitless horizon where he could fulfill numerous dreams. Dan's story, though filled with heartache, is a success story that will inspire anyone who has ever dared to dream big dreams.

* * *

Growing up Amish involves hard work and long hours. Most children begin doing physical labor before age five. The first chore ever given to Dan was to milk one cow a day. Since Dan was to help with the milking, he had to get up every morning at 5 a.m. While this was not a difficulty in the summer, the winter proved to be a different story. With the morning came the ritual of leaving the comfort of a warm bed. Dan would get out of bed quickly, grab his pants, and run for the living room where a hot stove fire awaited him. There, in the living room, he would get dressed while trying to evenly warm both sides of his body. Washing was a problem because many times the water would be frozen in the wash bucket.

Once Dan dressed, he would begin his morning milking. He not only had to milk one cow, but also help haul the milk to the milk station. Milk and hogs were the family's main source of income;

11

therefore, it was important for Dan to do his job well. While the men were outside working on the farm, the women were inside preparing for the morning meal. The Beachy family was poor, so breakfast usually consisted of sugar, milk, and a bread porridge. Sometimes the family would have fruit to eat. A simple breakfast food such as corn flakes was a treat to Dan and his siblings.

After breakfast, Dan would go out and continue his work on the farm. As he grew older, his work became more difficult. When Dan was eight years old, he took out his first team of Belgium horses in order to plow the fields that day. This work was incredibly strenuous, and many times the horses would drag him around as if he were a rag doll. On one particular occasion while Dan was harrowing the team of horses apparently spooked and began to run away from him. Dan fell down, and his clothes hooked onto the harrow making it almost impossible for him to grab for the reins. He bumped around the field, struggling to grab the reins. After a few attempts, he managed to grasp one of them. The team ran in circles until they tired and stopped to rest. Dan was lucky that he was not killed by the enormous animals.

After working all morning, the men and boys would stop and have lunch. The noon meal would be much larger than breakfast, for the Amish consider it the most important meal. Usually a meat along with potatoes, a vegetable, and bread was served for lunch, and once lunch was over, everyone would go back to work until dark. By about eight or nine o'clock at night, supper was served, which was usually a soup. Few hours remained in the day for any sort of amusement, but when supper was completed, the family went their separate ways. Dan liked to read, so to enjoy this simple pleasure, Dan would escape to his room. At around 10 p.m. Dan would go to bed, thus concluding an average day in the life of an Amish boy.

But the lifestyle of working hard on a farm was not the motivating factor that caused Dan Beachy to leave the Amish church, rather it was the abuse by his father and the strictness of the church. While his early years were not difficult, Dan's teen years proved to be mentally and physically hard. Being the oldest of fifteen children, Dan, many times, would be blamed for the mistakes of his younger siblings. As a result, Dan would be beaten severely by his father. S. B. would strike his son with whatever was at hand, usually leather tugs, or straps, sometimes even chains. The one instrument that hurt the worst was number nine wire.

Many times Dan was beaten because his father needed to vent his own frustration. While beating his son, S. B. would yell abusive language. Dan was determined not to cry, even if it took all his strength. The tears were hard to hold back because of the terrible pain he felt with each lash. As each strike made contact with his back, Dan would feel a jolt of pain that went from the point of impact to the tips of his toes. Only the anger he felt for his father helped him maintain control. Mustering up all his courage and strength, Dan would wait until either his father had left, or until he was out of his father's eyesight before he would show any emotion. Many times it would be Dan who would leave the scene of a beating, and all that he could do as he walked away was to attempt to control the shaking that began in his hands and worked its way through his body. Once out of sight, Dan would drop to his knees and let the tears flow. No sound came from him. Only tears were allowed to escape from his raw and cut body.

The abuse escalated until Dan decided that he must run away. Fortunately, Dan had an ex-Amish uncle who provided help in the form of allowing Dan to stay in his home. This uncle made S. B. promise never to beat Dan again, but though he made that promise, S. B. did not keep it. The physical abuse continued and with it came more mental abuse. Eventually Dan stood up to his father by taking from his father's hand the wire that was used for the beating. From that point on Samuel did not strike his son, but he would yell at him: "This will go home with you," which means that on judgment day Dan will be punished by God for disobeying his father. Standing up to his father made Dan feel good about himself because he knew that he had won a small victory. Though he was able to stop the physical abuse, Dan knew he would never be able to relax around his father.

The Amish culture does not encourage physical affection amongst its members. This added to the distant feelings Dan had towards his father. Never did he see his parents kiss each other or anyone else, nor did any family member express verbally any feelings of love. The only emotions the Amish show in public are sadness and misery because the Amish believe that the more sadness and misery one has on earth, the more happiness one will have in heaven.

Though Dan's relationship with his father was stressful and unloving, the relationship he had with his mother was quite good. M. B. could never step in between Dan and his father when Samuel was beating his son, but afterwards she was there to comfort Dan. What made their relationship strong was that they felt they could talk to each other and the other would listen. Their relationship was so good that after Dan had left the Amish, he felt that he could verbalize his love for his mother. Unfortunately, M. B. having lived all her life as Amish, could not break away from what she had learned about affection. She has never told Dan that she loves him.

* * *

From the time he was a child, Dan Beachy was always the inquisitive type. He liked to ask questions and learn about his surroundings. But growing up Amish did not bode well for Dan's questioning mind. Many times Dan would question an adult about scripture or about life, and he would be told that he would understand when he got older. His active mind also got Dan into trouble. When Dan was in the fifth grade, he made cigarettes out of sawdust for himself and a few friends to smoke. When recess came, Dan and his friends went out behind the woodshed to smoke the sawdust cigarettes. The first cigarette was lit, and the boys inhaled the harsh smoke that hit the back of their throats. To avoid being caught, the boys blew the smoke into a hole in the wall of the shed. Even with their precautions, someone smelled smoke and informed the teacher. Because Dan was the one caught with the cigarettes, he was the one punished. The teacher whipped him with a leather strap.

When Dan was older, he was placed in the ban for an incident that happened with a tape player. Somehow Dan and two other boys were able to obtain a tape player. They collected tapes of country music, but also they were able to procure blank tapes. Because their clothing was loose fitting and had large pockets, these three boys were able to hide the tape player in their clothing and tape conversations with others. Also, the boys would tape each other talking and making fun of various people, some of whom were the preachers in their community. Besides Dan and the two boys, other friends of theirs knew about the tape player, and eventually someone decided to snitch on Dan and his cohorts. Dan's own grandfather was the one who caught Dan with the tape player and tapes. The tapes were played before the members and the ministers of the church with the result being that Dan was placed in the ban for two weeks.

When someone is in the ban, they are shunned by their community and their family because they believe that the offensive person has given his or her soul over to Satan. While in the ban, the person must eat alone, stay at home from work, and he cannot have any contact with a person who is not a member of the immediate family. The shunned person can take things, such as a plate of food, from someone not being shunned, but those who are not in the ban cannot take anything from someone who is in the ban. This isolation is supposed to make the offender feel repentance. Usually when a person is in the ban, he is asked to perform a penance, which means the person stands before a group of church members and asks for forgiveness. If one of these members did not like the offender, then that member could deny forgiveness, and the person would have to continue in the ban until everyone is agreed to lift it.

* * *

For twenty years, Dan lived in the Amish community. At the age of seventeen, he became a member of the church, but he did this because of peer pressure. If a person does not join the church, then he is treated as if he were being rebellious, which brings much disapproval from the members of the church. At age seventeen, Dan began dating a girl, and they became a steady couple. But Dan became more and more unhappy with his life. Though he was growing older, the questions of his childhood were not being answered as the adults had told him they would be. Instead, more questions plagued him. Dan would see English farmers using tractors and wonder why the Amish had to use the horse and plow. From the time he was a child, Dan was perceptive, and he noticed the outside world. Things such as radios and televisions intrigued him, and Dan began to sense that he was missing out on something, but because he was rarely exposed to the outside world, he did not know exactly what he was missing out on. In addition, Dan began to question various scriptures, and the ministers would inform him that he should not be doing such a thing. Looking at the Amish tradition, Dan Beachy would question why breaking away from the church would be such a terrible thing since the Amish themselves broke away from a pre-existing religious group. These questions, the abuse from his father, and the sense of being limited forced Dan to look at his life and to re-evaluate what he wanted to accomplish. For six months, Dan seriously considered leaving the church, but it was not until his father beat him severely for stopping at the English neighbor's house to watch television that Dan made up his mind to run away.

Before Dan left the Amish he happened to find an old camera that was lying in a trash pile. Somehow Dan managed to get film for this camera, and he took pictures of various family members so that he could have a little piece of them to take with him to the outside world. He knew that once he left it would be a long time before he would see them again, and he knew that in the future he would not see them very often. Dan took pictures of a few friends and some of his siblings. Since his parents were such strict Amish followers, Dan was not able to take any photos of them.

Once Dan made up his mind, he knew that he needed to have a few things in order. One of those things he needed to have before he left was his birth certificate. Two weeks later on a Sunday in June of 1986, Dan left with his birth certificate and twenty dollars in his pocket. The plan was that Dan would go to singing that Sunday night and leave as soon as the singing was over. From the Sunday night singing, Dan went to a neighborís farm where he had once been employed. When he reached his neighbor's barn at two o'clock in the morning, he put up his horse and began walking away from his Missouri settlement, never to return as a member of the Amish. When asked if he was scared walking down dark roads into an unfamiliar town, he replied, "I was more afraid of what I left behind than I was of the future that lay ahead." Two hours later, Dan reached a small town in Missouri, where he went to the house of his ex-Amish aunt. The next day this aunt took Dan to a larger town for him to buy the things he needed. While shopping for clothes Dan was recognized by an Amish acquaintance who informed Dan's family where he was.

Once Dan's family knew where he was, they began to visit him. These visits were attempts to coerce Dan into returning. For several days in a row, the family hired a driver with a van, and with preachers and a bishop along they would cry and preach to Dan in an attempt to make him feel guilt, shame, remorse, and fear. Dan did not want to see these people, and he would try to hide from them because he felt so vulnerable.

Eventually the visits ended, and Dan was left to make a new life for himself. His integration into the English world was not easy, but Dan started his new life with a job working for Joe Burkholder. As an Amish person, Dan was accustomed to building barns and houses in a certain fashion and using certain equipment. Now that he was working in the English world, Dan had to relearn what construction work entailed, and he had to learn how to use power tools. Instead of helping with all aspects of building a structure, Dan had to acclimate himself to the concept that each person had one specific job and did only the job assigned to him. The first job was hard work and working for Joe was, at times, stressful because Joe was so demanding, but Dan succeeded in learning the English construction business.

Blending into the English culture was a challenge for Dan, who grew up speaking Pennsylvania Dutch. Many of the customs were strange to Dan. When he saw someone tip at a restaurant, he did not understand the point of tipping the person who brought the food, and he thought it a waste of money. Why would someone need a tip? Isn't she being paid enough? If not, then why not find a job that pays better? These were the thoughts that ran through Dan's head. Ordering food was new to Dan, for he had grown up in a culture where you go home to eat, and you eat whatever is placed in front of you. Once when he was ordering eggs, the waitress asked Dan how he would like his eggs prepared. All he knew to say was, I want them cooked and on a plate. Dan did not know that he could have his eggs fried, poached, or sunny-side up, rather he was used to having his eggs prepared and placed in front of him without being asked how he wanted them cooked. When looking at a menu, Dan did not know what items were served for breakfast, lunch, or dinner. Once at a fast food restaurant, Dan was looking at the menu and did not know what he was supposed to order, but also he was not familiar with the foods he was reading except for ice cream. So he proceeded to order ice cream, but since it was morning and only breakfast was being served, Dan could not order ice cream.

Within the first few months after leaving the Amish, Dan

started to teach himself how to drive. Of course he made mistakes, but eventually he had enough practice operating a vehicle that he was able to obtain a driver's license. One adventure of Dan's occurred at an intersection. Driving along, Dan did not notice that his gas tank was running low on fuel. As he entered the intersection, his car stalled in the middle because it had run out of gas. Not long after his car had stopped, a police officer came by and began questioning Dan as to why he was blocking traffic. Dan was petrified because the cop seemed to be so menacing, but once Dan explained what had happened, the officer relaxed and offered to help Dan move his car. The officer was so kind as to give his phone number and tell Dan to call him if he ever needed any help.

Besides becoming acquainted with the English language, new customs, and modern machinery, Dan became acquainted with such things as running water and proper use of a toilet. When he lived with the Amish, Dan did not know what it was like to have running water in the house. His first experience with a shower at the age of twenty-one was a delight to him, though it proved to be a bit of an adventure. When he went into the bathroom to take a shower, Dan did not know how to turn on the water. A friend showed him how to pull the knob to turn on the water and to twist the knob in order to adjust the water temperature. From there, Dan climbed into the tub, but he did not know how to get the water to go from the faucet to the shower head. Yelling to his friend, Dan asked how he could get the water to the shower head, and his friend told him what to pull. Now Dan was ready to take his first shower. When he pulled on the knob that would send the water to the shower head, Dan got a little surprise. All of a sudden water gushed out at him and hit him directly in the face. Because of the suddenness of the rushing water, Dan was taken aback, and he opened his mouth in surprise getting a mouth full of water. Coughing and sputtering, Dan felt like he was drowning. After the first few surprises, he knew what to expect and enjoyed the shower.

Getting used to pants with a zipper instead of a flap and buttons proved embarrassing at times when he forgot to zip his pants or when he accidentally got caught in the zipper, which can be quite painful. But soon Dan became accustomed to the English way of living.

* * *

After working for Joe Burkholder for a year, Dan went to work for Andy Miller. The next two years Dan worked for Andy, but after those two years he decided that he wanted to strike out on his own. He did sub-contracting jobs. This line of work led him to Charleston, South Carolina, where a hurricane had caused much damage to homes and businesses. Dan settled down in Charleston and took roofing jobs. While there, Dan met a woman, dated her for two years, then they married. Not long after they married, they moved to Missouri. Soon a son was born to them, but their marriage was not to last. After being married three years, Dan and his wife divorced, and Dan has custody of the son.

Today, Dan enjoys his own remodeling business which is successful enough for him to employ his own crew. He feels he has improved his life since leaving the Amish, and he is quite happy with his new life. As an English person, Dan can dare to dream of becoming financially secure and seeing the world. But even today, Dan is still in the ban and is not accepted by some of his family, especially his father. When he visits his family, he is able to visit with pride, and he lets his family know that he is proud of who he has become. These visits are few, though, because he is not really welcomed by his family. Despite being shunned and abused by the Amish, Dan holds no grudge. Deep down, Dan knows that the Amish people have been brainwashed into thinking that they are the true and only religion, and this attitude keeps him from feelings of resentment.

Dan does not regret his decision to leave, and he is willing to help those who also want to escape the confines of the Amish religion. While he is willing to help other Amish leave the church, he does not advise them one way or another because he feels that the decision to leave should be left up to the individual. For Dan, the decision to leave was not so that he could be rebellious, rather he left because he was tired of the hypocrisy, the abuse, and the oppression that his religion forced upon him.

Since leaving, Dan has been able to enjoy life without having to feel guilt or shame. With his new freedom, Dan sees many wonderful things in his future, like traveling to Europe and owning a nice home. These are simple dreams, but they are the dreams of a man

19

who has had to endure much pain and suffering in order to gain his liberty.

Chapter Three
Joni

The sounds of the sleeping farm lay heavy on young Joni as he began to drift off to sleep. The cool night air that drifted in through his partially open window carried with it the constant serenade of the crickets and the hush of the leaves in the trees as they rustled in the wind. On the tree limb outside his window was a hoot owl, asking the same old question: Who? and it seemed to Joni that the owl was talking to him—asking who he really was. Everyone had already fallen into the deep sleep induced from a day of milking cows and shucking corn—everyone except Joni.

Off in the distance, a noise began to invade his silent dream. It started out soft, like the hint of thunder after lightning; then it grew louder. The roar of it moved swiftly forward like a wave finally crashing. Closer and closer, louder and louder it grew until it was right upon him. Joni smiled, and listened to the car as it passed on the road outside, and then was gone.

Memories flooded back, and he recalled a day that was so clear in his mind that surely twelve years had not passed, but yes, they had. It was a sunny day, and he was five years old playing happily in the sandbox with a few other children. A thought of his cousin Ed was there, a man who could drive fast cars and do wild things like listen to the radio, watch television, and date English women. His cousin had left the Amish, and even at five years old, Joni knew that's what he wanted to do. The children hearing the blasphemous words, promptly told Joni's older brother what he had said. He in turn told their father, who gave Joni one tremendous spanking when he got home from his afternoon play, but the punishment did not daunt him.

Twelve years later, he was still dreaming about leaving.

On a normal winter's day, Joni rose with the animals at five oíclock as the sweet aroma of his breakfast teased his senses. Hurriedly dressing, he slipped into blue shirt, blue trousers, suspenders, boots, then rushed to beat his six brothers and four sisters to the outhouse behind the house. It was cold. All the way there he would hope beyond hope that the Styrofoam they put on the seat to make it warm was still in place. Later, gathering around the stove to beat the morning chill, waiting for breakfast, they would pray, as their father read passages from the Bible.

On most mornings, Joni's mother would have breakfast piping hot and waiting for them on the table: hot pancakes, sweet applebutter, liverwurst, and diced onions. The children would all be sure to take their fill, because it was a long time until dinner and after breakfast, chores began.

Milking was first on the list. About thirty cows occupied the farm and each person took four or five. With cold callused hands, they would work all morning milking the cows, putting out feed, and hauling manure.

As midday approached, the horses were hitched up to the wagon and taken to the corn field for the rest of the day's chore, husking corn. They pulled the brown husks from the corn, chaffing their chilled dry hands, looking forward only to the small respite of dinner. Breaking around noon, they would abandon their task and head for the house.

This was time when they could all take a moment to rest and warm up around the stove, if the weather was cold or wet. They ate potatoes and meat with apple or pecan pie for dessert. The children would eat as slowly as they could because they knew that right after they finished, it was straight back out into the cornfields where they would husk until dark. Once the somber cover of night set in, it was time to milk the cows for the last time. Soon it would be over, until the following morning, then it would be to do again.

Supper was never very heavy, a warm soup, some fruit, and cake. They would devour it happily, pleased that much had been accomplished for the day. For prayer, they would gather together and listen to their father, the bishop, read again from the Bible. Only then would the weary of mind and body see themselves off to bed, preparing for the day that was soon to follow.

April 20th, 1980 was not one of these days. It was a sunny, almost springlike, day. A good day for an adventure. Seventeen-year-old Joni had been asked to go help his older brother, Joshua, on his farm. At about 10 a.m., before he left, his mother noticed that five dollars had been taken from her pocketbook, and she confronted Joni about the missing money.

She came out and asked if I knew what happened to it, and I denied it. She asked me if I was going to leave, and I lied and said, No, because I didn't want her to know.

For a long time, Joni knew that he was not going to live his life under the restraints of the Amish. For twelve years he pondered the thought of leaving constantly. Ironically enough, the day he did choose to leave was not planned. With five dollars in his pocket, Joni set off for a new town and a new life. His spirits soared higher with every step that he took. The sun shone brighter, and the air was silky and sweet. He didn't know whether to laugh or cry, only to keep walking, no matter what was ahead.

Leaving the Amish was not a particularly hard decision for Joni. When he left, he had no idea what kind of world he would be stepping into, what kind of dangers would be waiting for him; he just knew he had to go.

Joni also had no concept of money. Amish children work all their young lives, but up until the age of twenty-one, they do not see the money that comes in due to this hard work. All the money goes directly to the parents, and the child never sees it. This is why Joni thought by taking five dollars from his mother's wallet, he was stepping out into the world a rich man.

Joni was the youngest of eleven children with six older brothers, and four older sisters. Out of all of the children, Joni was among three that decided to leave the Amish; two of his older brothers also chose the same path. They were children of an Amish bishop, and so had a greater obligation to portray perfection to the other children around them.

Joni explains it, "We were supposed to be the kids that were the good examples for other kids...people seemed to think you weren't supposed to make a mistake."

With these pressures placed on Joni, thoughts of the English

23

world began looking even better in his mind. Joni says, I saw something different in life. I had it in my head I wanted something different. Something different is exactly what he got.

Joni had heard of a man who would help people that were wanting to leave the Amish. His name was Gary Haynes, and he lived close to the Amish area. Rumor had it that he would find him a job and help him get some clothes. Like the rumors had promised, Gary did just that.

It had only been a few hours since Joni had left, but his brother was already aware of his actions. As Joni was leaving the Haynes house, his older brother met up with him in the wagon. He promised that as long as Joni came back with him, no one would ever know that he had even thought about leaving. The plan was to hide him in the hay in the back of the wagon and sneak him back into the community. Joni quickly refused, and left his brother there.

Once a little lamb has been lead astray, it is tradition in the Amish community to hire a driver, and pack up one or two van loads of family and church members and set out on a mission to save the wandering one. The van will show the wanderer exactly how much pain and heartbreak they are causing. The van showed up three days after he left.

As the first van load slowly pulled into the parking lot of the motel where Joni's new boss had set him up, the white doors of the van opened and out stepped his family dressed in black, as if they were going to a funeral. Joni filled his lungs with the thick air, and hoped that a small amount of strength would find its way into his body.

His family filed into his room and took the proper formation to induce guilt. The women stood solemnly in the back of the tiny room and began weeping deliberately into their pristine, white handkerchiefs. The towering men stood much closer. His father, the bishop, stood the closest. With Bible ready, the preaching began.

From familiar mouths came scriptures, threatening punishment. Questions that were never meant to be answered ricocheted off the walls, piercing his heart. The women began to plead with Joni, breaking off mid-sentence to grasp each other for strength, then fall back into weeping.

His parents were surely going to wither away now that their

baby was gone. Joni was surely going to spend eternal life in the bonds of fiery hell. The world itself would surely stop turning on its axis if Joni Petershiem did not come back to his faith and community.

He refused. With a courage that could only have come from the God he had reportedly turned his back on, he refused.

For hours this went on, until they saw that Joni was not going to be swayed, not that day. They left and did not return for two more weeks, hoping that homesickness would set in, and he would surely be ready to go. It did not work then, nor a year later, when they tried again.

He did miss his family at first and the stability of the farm, but when things began going more smoothly, the homesickness quickly subsided.

The English world was a hard and cruel place for a poor, innocent boy. He was terrified at first, but knew that he must stick it out. Innocence soon turned to common sense and he realized that the world was not such a scary place after all.

Joni found a former Amish friend named Eddie and they moved in together, making their room at the Redwood Motel a temporary home. They had jobs on a local farm. It was the exact same work that they had done all of their lives, but because they were there by choice and not by force, it did not seem so bad. They would see the money that they worked so hard for, and even get a little respect along the way. No, it wasn't bad at all.

After traveling only in a horse and buggy for seventeen years, the idea of riding a bike was absolutely thrilling. Joni and Eddie both purchased one, and rode them to work everyday. They slipped easily into their English clothes, and could not remember a time when they had been so very comfortable. They were quickly becoming members of their new community, living and working in the English world.

The thrill of riding a bike soon lost its appeal, though, and so Eddie and Joni did what any normal young men would do, they bought a car. It was like a dream come true, truly heaven on four wheels, and for only one hundred dollars! A Dodge Cornet, four-door, just what every man wants. The three were a perfect match: all a little out of the ordinary, all searching for a new life, all without a license.

Joni and Eddie bought the car from a very nice couple who told them that it was to stay exactly where it was until the car and the boys were licensed. The boys didn't get a license but the couple had already given them the keys; what came next was only natural.

Highway 151 was the perfect place to test out their new toy. The long gray expanse of road went on straight and flat for at least eight miles, ending in a dark gulf of night sky. With nothing around to witness except a few lonely trees lining the road, Joni slipped eagerly behind the wheel.

The steering wheel felt smooth and firm in his hands. and he caressed it with reined anticipation. His body molded to the seat perfectly, as if it had been made for him. With his right hand, he found the keys and clicked them over to produce a sweet purring from under the hood. The pungent odor of gasoline and exhaust filled the car, and he took them in like a child smelling hot cookies. His foot found the pedal as he shifted the car into drive, and took off.

10...20...60...80...mph, the Dodge sped into action. The wind whipped wildly through the open windows, snapping his hair into a frenzy. The sounds of the engine, the wind, and the night filled his ears so completely that he did not even hear himself when he opened his mouth and screamed. This was the dream; this was the moment; this was the freedom that he had wanted ever since he was five. Everything else just drifted away into the thousands of stars that lined his path.

Not long after that night Joni and Eddie decided that they were going to visit Joni's brother, who had also left the Amish. They packed some beer into the back of the car and started out on their road trip. It did not take too long for the boys to get a little rowdy.

They were at Joni's brother's house when Eddie decided he was going to make a side trip to see some friends. Eddie started to pull out of the drive, and Joni quickly saw that he was heading for something he had failed to see: a tree stump. Joni hollered out a shout of warning. Eddie saw Joni and thought that he was hollering because he wanted one of the beers that they had stashed in the back. So, Eddie, to be silly, pulled off quickly and soon met with the obstacle that Joni had been shouting about.

Joni ran for the car and got there about the same time that

Eddie had gotten out and moved around to the front. The bent and twisted front end grimaced at the two boys, and looked worse than it actually was. The extent of the serious damage was a broken tie rod. Not to worry, they had some wire.

It is amazing what a teenage boy is able to do to make his car run. Eddie and Joni were able to wire their tie rod, and a few other odds and ends back together. They did such a good job, in fact, that they decided to go ahead and finish their trip.

A little bit slower this time and a little bit calmer, they set off down the road. Along the way, Eddie decided he wanted to make a quick detour over to his cousin's. As they were nearing their destination, they came upon a steep hill with a very little bridge.

Eddie, realizing that he was going too fast, stepped on the brakes. Because of the wired tie rod the car veered slightly to one side when he pushed on the brakes. He lost control of the car and smashed right into the edge of the bridge, popping the hood and causing it to fly up. Feeling lucky to be alive after the events of the night, Joni and Eddie stepped out of the car. The hood was broken and would not stay down, but they simply wired the hood shut and went on, and this time they made it.

After a few more months of this treatment, the car could no longer take the tender loving care bestowed on it by Joni and Eddie. The boys soon cut their losses and moved on to the next vehicle. The Cornet got junked.

The next car that Joni and Eddie bought never did get wrecked. No, the transmission just went out on it. The only way that it would go was if it was in reverse. The last time Joni drove it was six miles backwards, out of town. This car, too, soon got junked.

As time went on, it seemed to prove that cars and Joni Petershiem just did not go together. Late one night Joni and Eddie had it in their minds to cause some harmless trouble. Well, no trouble is harmless, and only bad things can come from it. They got in their car and drove to their old Amish community. Over the course of this night, Joni's whole world would change.

There was not a cloud in the sky, only the bright diamond dusting of stars. The man in the moon even seemed to have a nice smile on his face as though the night would pass peacefully. Everyone in the small Amish community had long ago drifted off into slumber. For Joni and Eddie, it was the perfect opportunity to make some noise.

They started out riding around honking the horn, squealing tires, normal teenage antics. Then they tossed a few firecrackers into the barns and outside of the homes. Before the night was over, Eddie got into a fight with a man who was causing trouble for him and Joni. As the sun was coming up, Joni and Eddie were driving back toward town, this time as fugitives.

A couple of days later, Joni picked up the local paper and saw that his name was on the front page. He read slowly, taking in words like destroying and trespassing. With his heart in his throat, Joni quickly showed Eddie how they had made the news, and they discussed exactly what to do. They were afraid and on their own.

Eddie decided that it was only another ploy for the Amish to get them to come back. None of the charges were true, and no matter how scared he was, he was not going to give in. Joni's heart told him something completely different, and hearing from his father that if he came back the charges would be dropped, there was no doubt in his mind as to what he should do.

As Joni slipped out of his English clothes, he also slipped out of his freedom and his new life. With a heavy heart, he once again donned blue shirt, dark trousers, suspenders, boots, and had Eddie drive him back into the Amish community. The charges were supposed to be dropped because of his return, but reality and promises are very often two different stories.

It was a cool, overcast day when the two boys arrived at the Judicial building for their trial. Joni and Eddie were both being charged with destroying buggies, trespassing, and shooting firecrackers into the noses of horses. With fear eating at them, the two boys stood side by side, heads high, like two old friends should. Looking at them, though, you would not guess that they were old friends.

Joni had already slipped back into the proper attire of the Amish and stood next to Eddie in his Sunday best. Eddie, on the other hand, appeared to have lived in the English community his entire life, and wore the English clothes. They appeared to come from two different worlds, yet they stood close enough to let their shoulders touch.

Eddie's father approached him with his old clothes and told

Eddie that if only he would put on his Amish attire, the charges would be dropped. What kind of man has that much pull in an English court system? Who could be so cruel as to take these drastic measures to ensure a person's return to a life he hated? It would have been so easy to accept the neatly folded pile of clothes, but not the lifestyle that came with them. Eddie refused and looked past his father into the unknown.

The charges were unfounded and they were ultimately dropped to the lesser degree of trespassing for both boys. Because Joni had returned to the community he was given time served and released the very same day.

Joni found himself back in the same position he had worked so hard to get away from. He was immediately supposed to get back into the habit of rising at five and doing his daily chores. He was supposed to rejoin the religious ceremonies, and as his mother hoped, finally become baptized into the church. He was supposed to set a good example for the children who constantly asked him to tell stories of the English world. He was supposed to do a lot of things that he didn't.

Joni was never abused in any way, shape, or form, as some of the people who left the Amish communities were. He just always had dreams that there was a better life waiting out there for him. He can remember lying in bed at night and listening for the thick sounds of the cars going up and down the road. He remembers hearing stories of his cousin Ed and the happy life that he had found after leaving the Amish.

Looking around the dry dusty cornfield, Joni saw all the dreams that he had almost achieved being blown away by the breeze. He had to leave. He was not a member of the church, so he would not be banned, only shunned. He would probably rarely get to see his family, they would never tell him not to visit, but they would not really want him to. His mother would probably write letters and he could write her. These were all chances he would have to take.

He wished that he could leave the young Amish who had asked him about leaving a bit of advice. If he could, he would tell them this, It's up to you to leave if you want to, but you've got a lot to learn out here. You're on your own, and it is hard to leave your family at first. Go on and don't look back.

Joni, following his advice, never really looked back after that moment. He did, however, take a quick peek over his shoulder one day and saw the faces of those he left behind. Some looked very angry, some sad, others bewildered and confused. All were Amish, and most would choose to ignore his existence altogether.

Joni got back into contact with his good friend Eddie after he left the Amish, and they picked up right where they left off. They began doing carpentry work close to where they lived, and began making a life for themselves. When the itch got into them to move around, they took off for Texas, and worked in the oil fields. It was there that Joni got to spend some time with his two brothers who had left the Amish. Times were good and life was free.

But money began to dwindle and living from paycheck to paycheck was no longer working. Joni and Eddie soon parted ways, and Joni said another long goodbye to his brothers. Joni moved into a house five miles from his old Amish community.

It was a small white house appearing completely innocent on the outside, but what was inside told a different story. When the moon was full and the night quiet, the teenagers from the local Amish community would sneak over to the small house and for a few hours fulfill small imaginings of the English lifestyle, with the help of their good friend Joni.

Loud rock-and-roll music could be heard coming through the haze of different types of smoke. Couples would lock momentarily in forbidden embraces and make memories to keep with them through the next day. Glasses were filled and then quickly emptied of their intoxicating content. Favors of every persuasion from medical to material were asked of Joni, and sometimes he reluctantly complied.

It was no secret what was going on in the house, or who the Amish thought was to blame. Joni was a carrier of the evils of the English world and was quickly signing the children up to share eternal damnation through his powerful influence. It was not long before he was asked to leave.

To be a little difficult he refused, even though moving was not such a bad idea. It escalated to the point where the Amish began putting pressure on the owner of the house to get rid of the occupant. With a knock at the door and a shake of the hand, Joni was gone and pushed away into the real world once more.

It was a world where the guilty conscience of a young man began to weigh heavily. It was a world where the knack of swinging a hammer could bring big bucks. It was a world where Joni met the love of his life.

Her name was Sheri. She had long dark hair, lovely eyes, and a smile that gave Joni a lump in the back of his throat. She was so special, and for some reason God had seen fit to place her in Joni's reach. She quickly knew everything about him because he could tell her anything, and he did.

He told her about how hard it was when he walked away from his family, friends, and home; and she admired him for his courage. He told her about all the stupid things that he had done, and she laughed in spite of herself. And when he told her, I'm sorry for the crazy stuff I did. I hope they forgive me. I hold no grudges and I hope they hold no grudges. I meant no harm. I was just young. I didn't leave because of abuse or negative things, I just wanted to live my own life. It seemed like the stuff you weren't supposed to have was what you wanted, and you had to hide it and I got tired of hiding it.î She lost her heart in his sad eyes.

Secrets often slipped out over drinks, and sometimes the window to the soul opens just a little wider. He was so sincere in his words. We're not bad people after all. Maybe I might have been rowdy when I was young, but who wasn't? But it's not like I'm out here being all crazy now. I'm trying to make something out of myself. I want to be somebody.

When Joni made that statement he never even dreamed that the somebody he would become would have a life as wonderful as his. Sheri became his wife, and they reveled in the joy of being new-lyweds. They spent every moment together locked in a loving embrace which could only bring about one thing-a baby. The small house that could barely hold two was stretched to an abode for three.

The kitchen was too small to hold the three comfortably for breakfast, but they held their breath and made due. With their young son toddling there was always one more person to bump into in the hall. It was tiresome to deal with everyday, but the love that they shared made it easier.

One day, though, Joni and Sheri found a new house. On a hill overlooking a few acres of farmland and a little boy's natural playground, they made a new home. It came at just the right time because, once again, Sheri was expecting an addition to the quickly growing family.

Things could not get any better, or so Joni thought, until his boss and friend decided he was going to retire. Joni was extremely happy for his good friend and even happier to take over the business for him. Joni took over the construction company and all of the men.

Two years have passed in Joni's life since he took over the business. He has not learned all of the tricks of the new position yet, but has been very successful at what he is doing. Last year the construction company had so much business that they were turning people away.

He keeps his hand diligently on the hammer and works in the hot sun right along side of his men. It is a trait that he is thankful that he took away from the Amish. He not only was taught the trade from his former community, but also the pride that goes into and comes from a hard day at work.

Sheri and Joni are living happily with their two sons as they deserve after all they went through to get to where they are. Joni chose a hard road the day that he stepped off his safe Amish land.

To look at Joni, now, no one would ever guess the immense pain that once hid behind his dark green eyes. He seems shy, almost boyish, in his manner. His handsome tan face is hardly ever seen without a brilliant smile and a laugh that insists others join in. There is a past there, though, that even a successful smile cannot always hide.

The few chances that Joni was willing to take when he left for the second time have all come to pass. Due to the fact that Joni is shunned by the Amish community, anyone Amish, including his family, is not supposed to have contact with him. Over the years they have cut off their writing communication, for the most part. They speak only when Joni and his family come and visit. Joni was never told by his parents not to come, but he knows that his presence causes trouble and he tries to keep the visits limited.

By the telling of this story he is lifting a huge burden off of his chest. For the past seventeen years that Joni has lived in the English world, he has had to carry with him the guilt of his decision.

No matter how good his life was, there were always things in his past that weighed heavy on his mind. Because of this, he wishes to address the Amish community, not only the one that he left, but also all those that have been affected by choices such as his.

Joni is very satisfied with his life. He insists that if he had to do it all over again, he would not think twice before doing it. He went from a ninth grade educated Amish citizen to a local construction company business owner and English family man. Successful in business and family, Joni remains humble about his accomplishments. Yes he says, I'm very much satisfied with my new lifestyle. I've got a beautiful family and a good job. Everything has went pretty well for me since I got married and settled down.

Joni comes home now to a family that he loves and they love him. Their love is unconditional. They know all about his past and not only do they accept his decisions, but also they stand behind him. He does miss the family he once had, but would not give up the new family he has for the world.

Chapter Four

Ed

Springtime is a time of rebirth, of hopes and dreams. I guess that is about the best I know how to explain that gorgeous day when I was sixteen years old. I was always in trouble at home with my Amish family, especially my father. Seemingly, I could do nothing right most of the time. We labored very hard in the fields day in and day out. Every day was pretty much like the day before, arising before the break of dawn to accomplish the many farm chores, all manually, of course (the Amish way).

I had always known that I would make my exit someday to the outside world. The day that I ran away from home was a gorgeous spring day. My father was in a good mood, but I knew that was only temporary. Once again, I had gotten in trouble, and I knew he would be finding out soon. Perhaps I would be better off to make my exit while everything was going good.

Clueless about what the English world would hold, I bravely took off walking with seven dollars in my pocket. Everything we earned was turned over to our parents until we reached the age of twenty-one, but until then we were allowed no money.

I was wearing my black hat with a hole in the top of it, along with the traditional Amish garb—dark blue shirt and dark pants and brown coat. Just the clothes on my back was all that I left with. Later, I had to return those clothes for my younger brothers to wear. I walked about five miles down the road to a neighbor's house and paid her all of my money to take me another twenty miles down the road. I arrived at J.G.'s house, but he wasn't home, so I slept in his barn for a few days. J.G. was ex-Amish. The Amish really looked down on him because he lived so close to the Amish after leaving with his family. I moved into an old shed beside his house, sleeping between old mattresses before he finally came home about a week later.

The most difficult thing I faced by leaving was that I was so alone in the world without a family to go home to at night. That was such a scary time for a young lad previously surrounded by numerous family members, now to be totally engulfed by total quietness. As the darkness of the evening crept upon me, I cowered into the musky smelling mattress. What was that sound? How can crickets be so loud?

I wondered if I was being missed back home. I knew my brothers would be disappointed in me because they would have to fill in for me by doing my chores. Just think of that good homemade bread I'm sure Mama baked for supper tonight. My stomach growled with remembered anticipation for Mama's home cooking. I remembered tonight was meeting night, and all of the Amish families would be attending. I crept from my homemade bed that I feared would be rat infested. My feet found their way down the road a couple of miles. Remembering the cellar entrances, I inched along until my hands felt the cool jars of fruit and vegetables lining the cellar pantry. I could hardly wait to devour the stolen foods. My heart raced excitedly as I made it back to safety without being caught as a thief in the night. I would have been so embarrassed had I been caught stealing food, but I was hungry! The next morning, I hungrily ate the canned sausage and canned apples as I forced myself not to think about the family back home having a hot hearty breakfast. For supper, I opened a jar of green beans and finished off the sausage and apples.

This was the first time in my life that I was making decisions about what to eat and when. Previously, my meals had always been prepared and set before me at regular intervals. How strangely exhilarating it felt to be in control of my own destiny. I could eat and sleep whenever I decided! As my tired mind drifted into a restless sleep, I wondered what the future would hold for me. Even as I woke up to a chilly early morning, I felt no regrets for my new-found freedoms. Only the deathly quiet evenings reminded me of the absence of cheerful noise a large family makes on a regular basis. Every evening as I tried to sleep, my mind wandered aimlessly to my previous home life.

Yes, even us Amish kids were mischievous just like the English kids. I recalled the times that my brothers and I would slip out and go to (English) neighbor's homes and watch T.V. all night and smoke cigarettes. We would slip back home just in time for our father to call for us that it was time to get up, and we hadn't even been to sleep yet! To cover our tracks, we went on with our work just like we had rested the night before.

One particular night, some of us Amish kids were sowing our wild oats partaking of the English ways; we had slipped back home in the middle of the night. Just as my brother Jake got to the barn with the horse, we saw that our father had stepped outside to go to the bathroom. Jake was really quick in thinking that time. He slapped the horse on the behind, causing the horse to run into the yard. The dogs herded the horse back into the barn lot. The next morning at breakfast, my father mentioned that the strangest thing happened during the night, and he proceeded to tell about the dogs herding the horse back into the lot. He said it sure was a mighty strange thing to him. As he shook his head, I thought I would burst out laughing, but for Jake's sake, I was able to contain myself!

Most folks probably wonder why people like me run away from my Amish home and upbringing. I would say that decision was made on my part from a very early age, say five or six years old. For example, I was driving a three horse team (1 colt and 2 grown horses). Now that amounts up to about 5,000 pounds of horse against an eighty pound child. I couldn't turn the horses or stop them. The horses straddled a fence, went parallel with the road, and wiped out about a hundred yards of fence posts until they finally ran into a corner and couldn't go any farther. My dad gave me the beating of my life for that, and I can never forget it, as I still have scars from the pitchfork in my rear end because I couldn't stop those horses where he wanted them stopped.

That was just the strict Amish way of correcting their kids; he always dished out strong punishment. I certainly feel that I was an abused child, probably verbally as much as physically abused. Still the main reason that I decided to leave was not the abuse, which of course was wrong, but I felt that the Amish way was so hypocritical. For instance, it was allowed that we ride in other people's vehicles, yet we couldn't own or drive one. We could use the English neigh-

37

bors' telephones, yet were not allowed to own one. We could not own tractors, but when we worked for our English neighbors, we were allowed to drive the tractors. I could just never figure out the reasoning for all of that.

I always knew that I would leave, but it wasn't easy to do. The first time I tried to run away from home, I was about fourteen years old. I remember my mother crying and begging for me to please come back. I turned around and came back for my mother's sake; I couldn't stand to break her heart like that. However, I knew it was just a matter of time until I could escape.

I truly believe that the reason the Amish stay Amish, is that they are so unlearned in the ways of the world; they have such a fear to leave. They are taught that if they leave, they will burn in hell. I never joined the church, so that wasn't my fear. I feared more if I stayed than if I left. Just because I didn't join the church didn't matter to them, as I was supposed to know better than to leave. I was so severely punished even when I was innocent, that it just didn't matter to me anymore. I knew that I would get a severe beating whether I was guilty or not. I learned early on to start crying from the first lick because they were determined to make you submissive, forcing you to admit you were wrong whether you had actually done anything wrong or not.

We were only given an eighth grade education, so we pretty much had to stay and depend on the Amish community to survive. We were kept ignorant and unlearned, only taught survival within our own realms of life.

I just knew there had to be more on the outside life for me than being held back like a prisoner. Yes, had I stayed I would have always been a prisoner because that way of life just wasn't for me. I hold no hard feelings for my parents. I love them tremendously, as they were simply bringing me up the way they had been brought up. I know in my heart that my father and mother love me very much and would love to tell me that, but they are scared of what their Amish neighbors would say. I love them very much. My parents taught me a great deal about life, and I am very thankful for them. In fact, I feel that every good thing they taught me outweighs the bad tenfold.

In comparison to the English kids, I just feel very cheated. The average English father and mother spend leisure time with their kids, and the English kids have such opportunities: swimming, hunting, fishing, baseball, football, hockey, camping, sightseeing trips, ice cream shops, burger places, etc. The only activity the Amish kids know is work, work, and more work. I do not mean to say that we didn't have our homemade fun, but we were very isolated indeed.

My friend, Joni Petersheim, left his family about the same time that I did. We met up and decided to find ourselves gainful employment and live together in a cheap motel room. With our first pay, we bought bicycles for five dollars each to take us to and from our jobs as farm workers. Those bicycles were faster than the horse and buggies that we were accustomed to, but not as fast as we wanted to go. Even though we made very little money, we thought we had money to burn since we had never had the chance to have cash in our pockets.

We found ourselves purchasing an automobile that we paid all of a hundred dollars for. Of course, we didn't have much of a car for that amount, but it was really something for us! One time the transmission was in bad repair, but I couldn't afford to fix it; somehow I still drove it, even though it would only go in reverse. One time I drove it for fifteen miles going backwards down on old country road!

Another evening found Joni and me slipping into an Amish home via a ladder to the upstairs bedroom window. The three giggly Amish girls quietly slipped us in for a visit. We heard the father's footsteps outside the door. Quickly, I darted under the bed. There was barely room for me to squeeze myself under there, but I saw no other escape as Joni had hidden in the closet. The girls all leaped onto the bed for a stern lecture from their father. The conversation was about me! He was warning his daughters to stay away from that no-good boy that had run away from his Amish family. Oh, the pain that I endured as he raved on for a solid hour! The springs of the bed were cutting into me from the weight of the girls. Finally, the father's sermon ended, and Joni escaped the closet to help pull me from under the bed.

I was encouraged by an English driver for the Amish (H.P.) to return to my former life. He simply would not leave me alone. At the time, I was breaking horses for a living. H.P. reported me to the Humane Society that I was starving the animals. The Humane

Society came out and investigated, and of course, found nothing askew. H.P. kept telling me that it is a cruel world and he was going to keep dealing me misery until I went back home permanently.

The next incident, H.P. had the cops raid my house for drugs. Once again, after unfounded accusations, H.P. again confronted me. "This is a rough life! You need to go back. If you go back, I will leave you alone."

I called H.P. to come over, telling him that I was homesick. When he arrived, I did all of my talking with my fists. The police report stated that I would have killed H.P. had it not been for a couple of my friends present that pulled me off of him. That is the first and last time that I have ever been violent. I was so frustrated with his intrusions into my life; he just wouldn't leave me alone. After so many personal attacks on my newly chosen way of life, I just wasn't going to take any more from him.

H.P. then swore out a warrant on me. I dyed my hair blond, had it permed really curly, changed my name to Ed and moved to Texas. I was going to work for a construction firm as a laborer, and a social security number was required. I finally got one, along with my driver's license. Exactly one week after receiving my driver's license, I had my first altercation with the police.

One night I was in a bar with my girlfriend when a policeman approached and asked to see my driver's license. I was jailed for public intoxication, but the bottom line was, I was wanted for attempted murder with a deadly weapon, (H.P.'s warrant). The deadly weapon happened to be my feet!

When I went to court, my father brought my Amish clothing, and said that he would drop all charges if I would return to the Amish. Yes, the State even offered to drop all charges if I would go back! I was not about to make a deal with the Devil.

I had a pretty good lawyer, I think. The charges were dropped to a Class D Misdemeanor from the original attempted murder charge. I ended up doing ninety days in jail, with a one year probation. I also paid H.P.'s hospital bills, and I had to write to the judge every week for one year. Going in to this situation, I knew that I could end up with five to fifty years in jail. I was willing to take that chance versus going back to the Amish.

Growing up, my dad always said that if I was going to put my feet under his table, then I had to abide by his rules or get out. He was a bishop, so I really made him look bad when I left. Although I never joined the church, it was a negative reflection on him.

I feel like a lot of wonderful creative brains have been ruined, and ideas lost by refusing the Amish children an education. I think they think that if they keep them down, keep them confused, keep them convinced that they are wrong, to me it all boils down to a cult. I don't even think that David Koresch would have gotten away with his cult members not going to high school. To me, that makes the Amish a worse kind of cult than most people are aware of.

My feelings are that the Amish is nothing more than a dictatorship. Children are so brainwashed by the time they are four years old; they fear the outside world so much. The English world is portrayed as evil and sinful and a sure way of damnation to an eternal hell.

There are so many different Amish churches that I believe they all try to out-do each other. If they don't agree with something, they break away and start a new settlement. Some of them split away to become more liberal, and others break away to become less liberal. This sounds very confusing, having no reasoning at all as far as I am concerned.

I have an uncle that fought the way that some of the Amish were baling hay with motorized balers. The balers tied knots automatically. He fought it and fought it, and finally split off from the church and Amish community that he was a part of. The first thing that he did when he left, after starting his own church, was to go out and buy a motorized baler. He was asked how he could justify this technology that was newer than the motorized baler that he had fought so hard against. His response was that his new baler did not tie knots. Go figure!

Many Amish communities do not have indoor plumbing. I firmly believe that God gave us all common sense. He gave us brains to use and he wants us to use them. I just cannot understand what difference it makes to have water going into a barn or coming from a well if it goes into the house too. Apparently, they believe that if the neighbors see you doing something wrong, that is just the worst thing to them. The Amish are not stupid people. Most of them are very smart, but they are not allowed to utilize their brains. They don't

41

worry about what God sees; they just worry about what their neighbors think. In this instance, they don't know right from wrong; they just don't know the truth.

I could not and still do not understand why the color of my clothes, or the number of buttons on my shirt and pants could determine my destination to the place where I would spend eternity after this life.

When I was a young boy in my early teens, I stole a radio from the neighbor that I had worked for that day. Of course, I only intended to borrow it and return it. I walked three miles in the snow to return it. When I returned home with frozen feet, my father was waiting for me with a stick for my punishment. He told me that I could either take the whipping he was going to give me or sleep in the barn. I chose sleeping in the barn in the dead of winter before I took any more lashings from him.

Going barefoot was just normal in the Amish way of life. We were only given one pair of shoes a year. I remember herding the cows when I was only about five or six years old, and in order to keep my feet warm, I would jump from one place to another where the cows had been lying down. We even stuck our cold feet into fresh cow piles (manure) to warm them.

My oldest brother always got to pick the jobs that he wanted to do. I didn't have any choice because I was younger. I just got stuck with doing whatever I was told to do. My father would leave us working, and we had better have our chores done when he returned or else—you guessed it—another beating! He was always off visiting the neighbors while we were hard at work.

One day my brothers and I decided to play around instead of working every minute. We were sliding down the new tin roof on the hog barn. My little brother Jake was two years old, and he slid off and broke his arm. We told my dad that he did it by helping us get the horse in the barn. He would have probably broken our arms had he known we were goofing off instead of working like good little Amish kids in his absence!

My advice to those that consider leaving the Amish is to please do not forget where you came from and be proud of your heritage. I know that is very hard to do, but with every bad thing there must be something good. If you were abused in any way as a child, learn from it by being strong, and remember not to raise your own children that way. Above all, always remember the most favorite Amish saying, "He that knows good to do and does it not, that is already a sin." If you know that you are living a life that you should not be living, then for goodness sakes, leave the Amish and get on with your life. Life is what you make of it; God gives us the opportunities to take advantage of for the betterment of our lives and our children's lives.

I have certainly learned how to be an effective parent by showing love and respect, and it comes back to me tenfold! I am probably too lenient with my own children, which is not rare when one is trying so hard to be opposite of what they knew growing up. I know that I will always love my children unconditionally, regardless of who they are or what they become. I do not allow other's opinions of me to deter my obligations to my family; they are and always will be first in my life.

Many of the kids that did the same things that I did are now married in the Amish faith and walk around in clothes that hide their identity. They tell people how bad they feel about my lifestyle. The fact is, they are still, for the most part, doing the same things or worse now than we did when we were kids. They think it's okay because they are still Amish and their fellow Amish neighbors don't know about it.

The Amish faith taught me to be prejudiced. I always had a very low opinion of blacks. We were taught to believe they were all just niggers, that they could not be trusted and would steal a person blind. I have found that to be a great falsehood! Some of my good friends in later life have been black. It was a great revelation to me to discover that the blacks were able to do anything that white people can if given the chance and the same respect.

In retrospect, the same misconceptions were drilled into us about the English. We were taught that all English were very worldly people. The Amish believed the English to be just like a herd of cattle with no morals or belief in God. Thank God they were wrong about that too! I respect all religions and beliefs, and I feel that it is wrong to judge a person by their skin color or clothes they wear. What really counts is what is in their hearts. I believe there is good in most everyone.

Eighty percent of the ones that leave the Amish return for various reasons. Several have returned because they fear they can't make it in the real world. Others escape for a short time just for a taste of the English life, knowing full well they intend to return when their partying is over.

Others have joined the Amish belief to hide behind the Amish religion. Amish do not believe in violence or war; therefore, a number of young men decided to become Amish just to escape their duty of serving their country. That is one of the first things I did when I left the Amish; I registered for the draft. I considered it an honor and my duty. Although I was never called to serve, I would have gladly defended my freedom.

The Amish communities are far from perfect. I am sure it would amaze the English to know what goes on behind closed doors. For those who are less fortunate, there is criticism and ridicule, and among those more fortunate or wealthy, there is jealousy and envy with each other. If you want to hear all the dirt or other news, then attend a quilting session at one of the Amish homes, or attend an auction. Gossiping is a favorite hobby of the Amish.

What a shocker this will be for those who think the Amish have such a perfect life. For myself, the only amazing fact that I have mentioned is that eighty percent that leave the Amish, return!

Our parents were so strict that they went beyond the limits of reasonable punishment. My second oldest sister, who was about eight or ten, was beaten so severely that my father damaged her eye. This was all over something she didn't ever do. My father was determined to make her admit to doing something for which she was not guilty. She was taken to the hospital to have her eye examined and repaired.

The Amish definitely get away with so much that is wrong just because of their religion! They think they are not bound by the laws of the country that punishes those who do wrong to their children. Amish want nothing to do with the law or the court system.

Despite the abuse that I experienced as a youth, I have overcome my situation because of a determination to make something of myself. I bummed across the country working odd jobs here and there after I left the Amish in 1979. I worked on cattle farms for awhile, then became a welder's helper. I started out as a laborer in a construction company, then learned welding on the job. All of my work skills have come from on the job training.

In 1983, I met my wife in a bar. I'm really not proud of the fact that this ex-Amish met his wife in a bar. On the other hand, I am not ashamed of it either! We married in 1985, and started a family shortly after (one son and one daughter). Right after we started a family in 1989, I started my own fabricating business.

My business fabricates metal and steel by building a line of equipment from pulp paper machines, railroad car dumpers, transfer belt conveyers, drag chain conveyers, and steel mill pollution control systems, along with computerized chipper infeed systems.

I feel very fortunate to have climbed the ladder of success despite only an eighth grade education. This shows what determination and a lot of hard work can do—it doesn't matter where your roots were or what happened to you. People can overcome and be successful if they wish to and can maintain a determination in order to make something of themselves.

Every year I attend an ex-Amish reunion. We have a great time socializing, what with a wonderful spread of food. I have the opportunity to see some actual blood kin that also left to better themselves. I have cousins that are lawyers and nurses—just a wide variety of lifestyles are represented. We have a common bond amongst us; we have not and will never forget where we came from. It is great to get together and see how, though stunted with an eighth grade education, so many have been really successful in life. We play volleyball and have a great time together. The reunion begins on a Friday and goes through Monday with an attendance of 200-400 people from everywhere.

I cannot stress enough the importance of an education. Obviously, the others that left the Amish felt the same way, as the majority found the opportunities to continue their education. Personally, I would love to continue my own education, but have not found the time to fit it into my busy schedule. However, my goal is to study with my daughter when she reaches the fifth or sixth grade, then earn my G.E.D. certification. I certainly hope that my own children will go to college after they graduate from high school. We will cross that bridge when we come to it. They absolutely must complete high school, which is more than I had the opportunity for when I was a child.

My oldest brother Eli is still Amish. I seldom talk to him, but hear from him through others. He is very well respected and has been very successful in his life.

A younger brother, Jake, left about seven or eight years after I left. He eventually found me, and we now work together as partners in our fabricating business. We employ about twenty-two people including a full office staff.

My life had been far from easy, as I have experienced a lot of setbacks and disappointments. My dear wife's murder in September of 1994 has been the most difficult of all. We were separated and were in the process of reconciling when she was murdered. There is still an open investigation into her death, so I cannot elaborate on any specifics at this time.

I loved my wife very much, and I felt like my world ended when she was murdered and I was left alone with two small children to raise. At the very lowest point in my life when I felt like I had no one at all, my mother came to be with me. I will forever be grateful for her coming to my rescue. Just knowing that I had her love and support during the lowest days of my life meant more to me than I can put into words.

I still visit my parents about once a year. They are actually very glad to see me, but they are so worried their Amish neighbors will see me there and get upset, so they are relieved when I leave a couple of hours later. Not all of my family (brothers and sisters) will talk to me; I am shunned by most of them. I still love them in spite of their ways; I figure they have a problem, not me.

I hope that my story will be an encouragement to those that are miserable in their life. I would consider this my greatest accomplishment: telling my story for others to realize that their dreams can become a reality. Do not be brainwashed into believing that you are going to hell just because you are not living by someone else's standards. My greatest advice that I feel is truly worthy for anyone is to read the Bible and believe it. Don't listen to the Amish. The Bible will tell you how to live and what to do in all situations.

I am very happy now. I have recently remarried a wonderful woman. Linda and I met at a football game in which my son was playing. I am so grateful to have met another wonderful woman to be the love of my life. Linda has a fourteen year old son from a previous marriage, and she brings with her a mother's love and understanding. My two children need this in their lives, and Linda's son needs a man to help guide him and to be there for man-to-man talks. It is as if all the pieces of a puzzle have come together. When I would leave work before my marriage to Linda, I would pick up my children at the baby-sitter and go to an empty house. Now, I leave and go home to my wife and our children. My house is now a home. It is complete.

I would recommend having more than seven dollars in one's pocket. But then again, I guess that's what makes my story so remarkable. A sixteen year old with no concept of money, so naive in the ways of life—who would have ever thought that he would become the owner of his own company? One might think of it as a rags-to-riches story. I call it being successful because of a determination to change my situation.

Chapter Five
Manny and Johnny

All they wanted was what most normal American boys want: a radio, a car, some freedom. But Johnny and Manny were born Amish. They didn't choose that lifestyle. They were born to it. Manny, whose real name is Emmanuel, was the older of the two, and he left first. He was twenty years old when he left the Amish. He was a member of the church, so he is now under the ban and shunned by the Amish. But Manny attends a new church now, and he doesn't miss their way of life. Johnny left when he was seventeen. He was never a member of the church, so he is not officially under the ban, but he too is shunned; both have felt the cold shoulder of the Amish.

Johnny remembered putting his head under the pillow at night to listen to a little radio that he had managed to buy with tips, extra money that the English slipped to the children because they knew they weren't going to get to keep any of the money they were paid. There are child labor laws in this country, but the Amish don't abide by them. Many Amish children work as hard as any adult, but they aren't allowed to keep any of the money they earn. They must "pay off their age." By the time Johnny was ten years old he was breaking ponies. He was one of the best. And he was a darn good farm hand. But all of the money Johnny earned went to their father, who decided how it would be spent. None of it was spent on the things that most children long for. But somehow Johnny squirreled away enough money to buy that pocket radio, and somehow he managed to purchase it without his father or anyone else finding out about it. At night, late, when all the rest of the family slept, he would listen to it down low, and it was like a ticket to another world — the English world — the outside. He wanted to go there someday, stay there forever. He was only a child, but he knew, even then, that he wanted to live in that other world. He could see it. It was right there, so close he could reach out and touch it, and yet he was not a part of it. Whenever he went into a store with his mother or father, he felt self conscious about his Amish clothes. He felt like the English were staring at him. He hated it. He wanted to be like them. He wanted to wear tennis shoes. He wanted to work for himself.

Manny started helping his father plow when he was five years old. He would drive the horses across the field, and his father would pick up and put the plow back down. Manny remembered watching his father as he walked ahead of him, plowing. By the time Manny was eight years old, he did the plowing by himself. It would take him all day to plow an acre. He stood leaning against the old plow, listening to the heavy breathing of the horses, and watched his English neighbor plowing with a tractor. Through the sweat that dripped into his eyes, he watched as the English neighbor plowed twenty acres in the time it took him to plow one. Every muscle in his sturdy little body ached. It made him so angry. Why did he have to work so hard, when there was an easier way to do it? Why? It didn't make sense. And when he didn't do it fast enough to suit his father, he got a whipping, a beating actually with a razor strap. That wasn't an unusual occurrence. His father would whip until he was satisfied, until he got his anger out. It wasn't fair.

One day Manny had an idea. He climbed the fence and walked across the field to his English neighbor's. He walked right up to him, and the man stopped his tractor, leaned down and said, "What can I do for you son?" Manny said, "I was wondering if you could plow my field for me at night while everyone's asleep." The man just laughed and said, "When your father asks me, I'll plow it." It had seemed like such a good idea to Manny, but now he was worried that the man might tell his father. He knew what would happen to him if he did. His father wouldn't like it one bit and another beating would be in order. For days, he lived in fear that the neighbor would tell his father what he had asked, but he never did.

Johnny wanted to drive a big truck. For as long as he could remember he had been dreaming of driving an 18-wheeler. Did that make him a sinner? He wanted to leave the Amish; his brother

Manny had already gone, but his parents said Manny wouldn't go to heaven. No one got into heaven except the Amish. He saw the English way of life, and it fascinated him; it was all that was modern: cars, televisions, cameras, radios, computers, movies, hot-dogs! What were they like? It didn't seem fair that he lived in the United States of America, yet he was forced to live like he was in some backward, third world country. He wanted his own car. He wanted to work for himself, and keep his money. He wanted to be free, really free, the way the English men were free. He started wearing his Amish hat turned up like a cowboy hat, but got into trouble for that. His father watched him more closely since his brother Manny had left the Amish.

There had been big plans in his household for weeks. At seventeen, the time had come for Johnny to start taking instructions for baptism.In order to join the church you must take instructions for baptism.In a room upstairs you take classes every two weeks from the bishop, ministers, and the deacon.You take nine classes or more, depending on how many the church elders decide you need. After these classes are done, you are ready to be baptized, thus making you a member of the church Church was held in his own home because his father was a minister, and he knew they would all be expecting him to join the class of young people the next day. He imagined their faces, their stares and whispers if he didn't do it. Still, he knew he couldn't do it. That night, he left his family and the Amish way of life behind. He climbed out of his bedroom window with a little over a dollar in his pocket, and his Amish hat defiantly folded up like a cowboy's, and he never looked back. At the end of the road, his X-Amish friends were waiting. He went to his brother Manny's house and stayed there for two nights. Then he went on to his sister Mattie's house, where he got a job working with his brother-in-law-Noah. Noah drove a delivery truck and Johnny started going along with him to help out. The Amish caught up with him one day as he and Noah were making a delivery. They physically tried to drag him out of the truck. They begged and pleaded with him to come back, but Johnny said, There's no power on earth that could drag me back to the Amish.

Manny joined the church, not because he really wanted to, but because it was expected of him, and if he wanted to associate with the other young people, it was a requirement. The night before Manny left the Amish, his father took him aside and said, "The bishop wants to see you." Manny went over there, and the bishop told him he was going to excommunicate him and put him in the ban the next day. He had been seen driving a neighbor's truck. So Manny went to one of the neighbor boys and asked him if he would wait for him outside the church the next day. When they kicked him out, he walked out of the church alone, and got into the truck down at the end of the lane with his English friend. He had $0.76 in his pocket. He had only the Amish clothes he was wearing. His friend drove him thirty miles south to the nearest city. Then he got out of the truck, and just started walking. He walked around just looking at the world, until nightfall. Then he found a clump of trees, and lay down beneath them to sleep. On the second day, he walked some more. He just walked and walked until he saw an English woman in her front yard laying sod. He introduced himself, told her his situation and asked her if he could do some work for her. He hadn't had anything to eat for over 48 hours. She told him he could finish laying the sod for her. He did it; she paid him, and he went to a Taco Tico. He had never been in a restaurant like that in his life — the lights, the people; it was very strange to him. After he ate the food, he was sick. He had never eaten spicy food like that. He had nowhere to go, and very little money, but he was not afraid. He went back to his clump of trees and slept there again. The English lady turned out to be a God send. Her son had just got killed in Vietnam so she gave Manny his clothes. They happened to be the same size. She hired him to do more work for her that summer, gave him the money to pay two months rent on a trailer and then introduced him to a contractor who hired him full time.

Manny spent some time sowing wild oats after he left the Amish. Like many young Amish men, he had repressed his normal urges for so long, he went a bit wild when he was free from the restrictions of the community. He drank; he smoked; he even did drugs. "For ten years, I lived to drink and smoke," Manny recalled. Manny helped to organize the X-Amish reunion. It was one big party, a celebration of freedom. He doesn't attend the reunions anymore because he doesn't want to be around all the partying. Sometimes he stops by just to say hello to some of them, but he doesn't stay long.

Johnny and Manny came from a big family. There were thirteen brothers and sisters living. Of those thirteen, four are now X-Amish. Manny left, Mose, Mattie, then Johnny, and finally a younger brother Joe. Their brother Mose stayed out for five years, but he married a former Amish girl, and they went back to the Amish together. Mattie has good reason to leave. Her father abused her; she was pregnant by an Amish boy named Noah from another community, and she wasn't married. She and Noah left, Noah in July and Mattie in October. They got married in October and had three children during the thirteen years they stayed out. Then Noah made the decision to take his family back to the Amish. Mattie couldn't go back to the Amish life; her children were not raised Amish, so she looked to her brothers on the outside for help. She took her children and went to Johnny's house. Johnny remembers, I had to physically throw Noah out of my house. Noah even kidnapped their son and took him back to the Amish. She got a job at the hospital until her brother Manny bought a bakery and she managed it for him. She obtained a divorce and got sole custody of her three children. But it wasn't just family members who looked to Johnny and Manny for help.

In the years after he left the Amish, Manny married three times. "I married the first English girl who gave me the time of day," he said. "And that lasted all of six months." The Amish go to an Amish school only through the ninth grade, and the ninth grade is only on Fridays to learn the German they need to read their Bibles. He met a girl who was attending college in his town. He married her and promised to put her through school because education was important to him. The marriage didn't last but Manny kept his promise and finished paying her way through school Then he met the woman who would change his life. Her name was Shiela. She attended the First Assembly of God Church. Her mother and one sister was a minister and Shiela was raised strictly Pentecostal. Manny started going to the church with her and fourteen months later they were married. At first it was strange to sit and listen to a woman preach, but today he says "They can preach as well as any man." Both he and his wife are very active in their church. The Amish believe that only they are going to heaven, but Manny now believes that only the blood of Christ will save — belonging to a certain denomination doesn't get you into heaven.

Manny tries to spread the word of Jesus Christ to other X-

Amish, including his brothers, but he says, "They are the toughest ones." The Amish have had religion forced on them all their lives, so when they leave many of them do not want religion at all — Johnny falls into this category. When asked what religion he is now, he laughs, and says, "Mountain Man."

Both of them were hard workers, and they wanted to succeed. They wanted to make it in the English world. They were determined not to go back, and neither of them ever did. Manny tried his hand at numerous careers. He was a deputy sheriff; he drove a truck for awhile; he even worked as a dance instructor. Eventually he and his brother Joe started their own construction business.

Johnny does construction too, working as a framer. But he prefers to work on his own. "I work for myself now," he says. He calls himself a workaholic, yet Johnny is also a sportsman who loves to hunt big game. He hunts bear and wild hogs in Arkansas and goes deep sea fishing in Virginia.

Manny and Johnny have tried many different things since they left the Amish, but one thing has remained the same: they have always been willing to help other Amish make it out. The brothers are known in the Amish communities across the nation. Many a sermon has been preached against them. Still there is a steady stream of Amish young people, arriving at their homes in Columbia, seeking refuge and help. Johnny says, "Some of the Amish would rather something tragic occur than to know they come to me for help." This is because with Johnny's or Manny's help, the young Amish often succeed in leaving. They often make it in the English world, and then they don't return to the Amish. The Amish would rather that their young people find the English world as frightening and evil as they have always been told it is. Johnny and Manny and others like them form a network — a little like the underground railroad. There are people who can help a runaway make it on the outside. Other X-Amish who have made it out the hard way are there to help make it a little easier for the young Amish who want to leave. Some of them come out for only a short time and then go back. Some of them never go back. They are the X-Amish.

Chapter Six
Mattie

Growing up in the Amish community was like living on the outside of a world that you were a part of and yet isolated from it, not so isolated, though, that you are not aware of how different the lifestyles are. As a young girl, I would dream of what it would be like to live on the "outside." I had a deep yearning inside, and I knew that one day I would become part of that world. I wasn't sure how and didn't know when, but I knew I would taste the outside someday.

The Amish are raised to work hard without the luxuries of a modern day world. My family lived in a very impoverished community. There was no electricity, no running water, no inside plumbing of any kind. In order to prepare a meal, a fire had to be started in the house and there wasn't so much as a fan to cool things off. You had to prepare three meals a day in the same fashion. It was extremely difficult. Not all of the Amish communities are just alike. Some of the surrounding communities had running water, and there were even some who used propane gas to cook. It would depend on who was in charge of your particular community. Even in the Amish communities, it was who you were and who you knew. So unfortunately, the case community where I was raised did not have anything close to a modern convenience. According to today's standards, you could say the work we had to do was slave labor. It was all so extremely physical. It required a lot of endurance. Everything we did was powered by human beings, except for the animals that were used to pull things such as a plow and the like.

There were thirteen children in my family. We all learned at an early age about hard work. No one was exempt from doing their share of the work. There was no discrimination between sex or age. There was so much to be done and it was expected that you would accomplish those tasks you were responsible for on a daily basis. Since I was second to the oldest, as far back as I can remember I was busy helping with the younger children. I had other responsibilities too, such as milking cows, feeding the chickens, and anything else I was told to do. My life didn't afford the luxury of relaxing or just having a good time, rather it revolved around work in some form or fashion. Sometimes the only thing that kept me going was the dream I had of living on the "outside."

My memories of my childhood were, for the most part, unpleasant. I worked very hard as a young girl. I was taught how to cook, sew, clean, and care for children. There were some jobs we worked separate from those of our immediate family chores. We would be paid a minimal salary for these jobs. Of course, we never saw any of the money we made, instead it went directly to my father to use as he saw fit. By the time I was a young teenager, I was quite familiar with every aspect of mothering and taking care of a household. Amish girls are raised to be very domestic, and mothering is not a choice you make, but it is what you do. As a matter of fact, Amish women are not allowed to make any choices; they are told what they are to do and they do it. They do not have a voice in anything really-definitely not in the church congregation, and they are allowed to say very little about anything concerning the matters of the family.

I do not have many fond memories of my childhood. There was a definite lack of love and affection. These were not part of our daily routine, not even so much as a hug a day. I believe we all have an inherent desire for affection and nurturing from our parents. But when a child is denied any form of affection from their parents, it causes immeasurable harm, deep scars which cannot be seen by the naked eye. In my own personal experience, I was terribly confused about love, sex, affection, and what was appropriate and what was not appropriate. Nothing was ever clearly defined for me. I doubt my parents ever experienced a display of affection from their parents either. I believe that I have been searching for something most of my life, and all the while I do not have any idea what I have been searching for. Without even knowing what hit me, I became a product of what I experienced growing up. My parents have passed on to their offspring those traditions they experienced. The Amish doctrines and traditions were embedded deeply into their souls. I can see now that it is such a mind game, one of extreme control. It is almost impossible to develop a mind of your own when you live under the hand of the Amish.

I lived most of the early years of my life in fear, fearing what would happen to me or what I would have to do if I were caught doing something wrong. This fear caused me to hide and seek a lot. I so desired to enjoy my life, but didn't dare let anyone know what I was doing. The threat of being found out was always looming over my head. If I did the least little thing incorrectly and got caught, I could be severely punished. Even though I was Amish, I was first and foremost a human being who had feelings, desires, and naturally I was curious about everything. Especially those things I was told I could not do. I wanted so desperately to experience life. I wanted to have fun, after all I was just a child. But under the Amish roof, nothing was allowed, so we had to sneak around and experiment with many of life's forbidden pleasures. I was very good at it too, I rarely got caught. When I did, the punishment was severe.

My father was a man governed by his emotions. He was a violent man with quite a temper. He was prone to fly off the handle without a moment's notice. It was not at all out of the ordinary for him to explode into fits of rage. All of us children suffered from his wrath. We were taught to obey and respect our parents, and we did obey. Not one of us children would dare confront him. My mother was not allowed to say much about his behavior. In the Amish communities, the man of the house is the head of the household. My father took full advantage of his authority. He would excuse his own behavior by using manipulative tactics. When his back was up against a wall, or he was faced with a situation he didn't know quite how to respond to, he would threaten to go into the woods and take his life. Of course, as children we didn't know how to respond to his threats. Certainly, we did not want to feel responsible for him taking his life. So he was most successful in his efforts to control us. My father was not a man any one of us wanted to cross.

Early in my life, it became quite apparent to me that my father had a special affection toward me. He would tell me how I was his little Matthew, after the apostle in the Bible, and how he was so very fond of me. It never made any sense to me. He was a preacher in our church, and he would preach sometimes about how it was wrong for boys and girls to do such things as touch each other and go even farther than that. It was wrong in the eyes of God. And yet, he would do these very things to me, his daughter. He would also manage to be alone with me in the barn, and then he would try to molest me. I instinctively knew something was not right, but I didn't know what to do about it. I would resist him as much as I could. He always told me that if I said anything to anybody he would deny it, and of course no one would believe me. They would believe him. He never got much further than kissing and grabbing, and I would fight him off. Sometimes he would get carried away. One time in particular, he got very forceful, and I kicked him right where it hurt. I did not expect the drastic results that followed. It was the only way I could get away from him. I was not going to let him go all the way with me, but I think he would have if I had not fought him off. It just never felt right to me, even though I didn't fully understand what was going on. We just never discussed anything of this nature in my family. I tried talking to one of my sisters about it once, and she said Mother probably already knew. She said we should not be talking about it. It's kind of strange, but after I kicked him, he never tried anything else with me. I suspect he moved on to one of my sisters. I did try to warn them, but it did not do any good. There wasn't much they could do about it either.

Life did continue even after all of the experiences with my dad. I never mentioned it to anyone else again. It just was not worth it, and no one would listen. The next encounter of a sexual nature I would experience was with some of the younger boys. At times I worked for families as a hired maid, when they had a baby or needed extra help. Some of these families had boys about my age. They would sneak into our rooms after dark, and we would just experiment. It was not a forceful experience, rather it was consensual. I liked the attention, feeling special. But it didn't mean anything more than that to me or to them either. In the Amish community, you are dictated to, not talked to, so sex was not explained or even mentioned. It was whispered about amongst the younger ones and scorned in church by the elders.

In my private times, all I would dream about was the outside.

**Amish Church Service
in a barn in Missouri**

**Amish people enjoying attending auctions,
it's a time to catch up on the latest gossip.**

**Young George Yoder in middle
with unidentified Amish friends.**

George & Lydia Yoder and family.

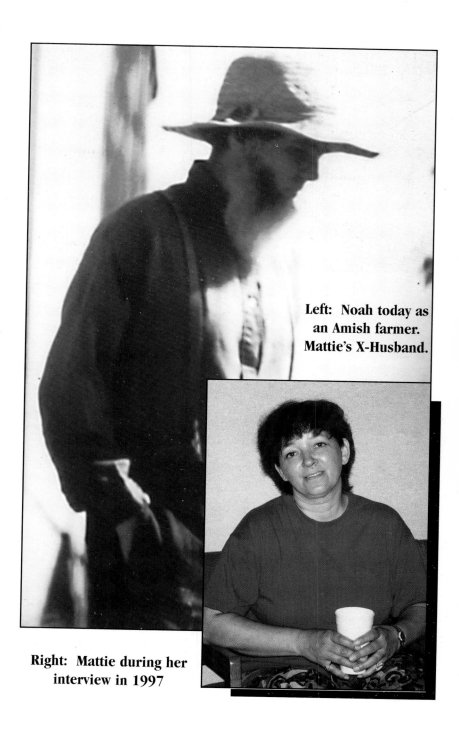

Left: Noah today as an Amish farmer. Mattie's X-Husband.

Right: Mattie during her interview in 1997

Above: Nebraska Amish Bishop at the National Steering Committee in Lancaster County, PA.

Left: Amish Bishops at the Fall meeting in Wisconsin.

Group of Amish Bishops and Ministers at the National Steering Committee in Lancaster County, PA.

Jake & Ed
Two brothers at work.

Joni & Ed together again,
Ed's wedding day.

Ed & Linda's wedding day with Ed's children,
Linda's son, and the minister

An Old Order Amish home in Kentucky.

An Old Order Amish home in Kalona, Iowa.

A younger LeRoy dressed in his Amish clothes.

LeRoy & his Fiance, Misty on vacation in California.

Neu Leben Writing Staff
Sue Neagle, Jennifer Wade, Michelle Coleman, Jennifer Hardy, Meredith Johnston, Tonya Parsons Cesler, Daniel Curry, Marilyn Greer.

**Mannie during his
interview in 1997**

**Johnny at his
interview in 1997**

Joni, Sherri & their two boys.

**Old Order Amish father teaching his son the
Amish way of farming near Clark, Missouri.**

**Jake and Edna Sehmucker,
a former Amish couple using modern Horse Power**

The X-Amish Reunion is attended by 200 to 400 former Amish & is held yearly over Memorial weekend in Columbia, Missouri.

Two X-Amish men are holding a flag which some X Amish use to symbolize their belief today.

**Joe & Rachel Schrock's family.
Several children are not pictured.**

Joe & Rachel Schrock's family just after they left the Amish.

Above: Dan with his sister, just before he left the Amish.

Right: Dan at his interview in 1997.

**Amish group checking out a stream
during an outing in the woods.**

Old Order Amish children at play in Kentucky.

Glen & Ida Yoder family.

**John & Matti Bontrager
Ura Yoder's daughter
& son-in-law.**

Levi and Miriam Yoder family.

Ura & Edna Yoder in their Amish clothes.

Ura & Edna Yoder at their son's home in Missouri 1997.

**A young Amish girls work is never done.
Using old time push mower in Missouri.**

A 12 year old Amish boy working a corn field in Missouri.

Old Order Amish going to town in Munfordsville, Kentucky.

Old Order Amish family on an afternoon outing in Kentucky.

Left: Amish Bishop and Wife along a country road in Missouri.

Below: Amish brother & sister gathering corn in Ohio.

Old Order Amish School, still used to this day in Missouri.

**This Amish school is closed for the summer.
A local Amish farmer will let his cows graze on the
tall grass but come fall, the grass is cut and children
will play at recess around this one room school.**

In my private times, all I would dream about is the "outside" world. I was looking for that right one to marry. I desperately wanted to get away from home. Marriage would give me the opportunity to do just that. I could start house keeping for myself. The day did come when I caught a glimpse of someone who seemed to trigger something inside me. It happened while I was visiting some friends in another community. There was this man or he may have just been a boy at the time, but he looked interesting to me. So I set out to get him to notice me. I finally did get his attention. His name was Noah. Before it was time for me to leave and return home, we had been properly introduced. This was just the beginning. Once the ball was rolling and we had gotten acquainted with one another, we did in fact end up in a dating relationship. This dating relationship lasted about four years, just a little longer than a typical dating relationship. The Amish even set standards about dating and how long that should last, then the announcement of marriage; everything had guidelines. Peace means following those guidelines. Since Noah lived in another community some distance from my home, we didn't see each other a great deal, but did manage to get together from time to time. In between visits, we would correspond through the mail. This was somewhat awkward as my father would always screen the letters we wrote to each other. We had to be very careful about what we wrote. Since it was a rather lengthy courtship, I wasn't sure if it would finally end up in marriage, but certainly hoped that it would. We had been dating for quite an unusual amount of time, by Amish standards that is. During the times when we managed to be alone, we had become sexually involved. Since we did not see each other on a regular basis, I was quite shocked to find out that I was going to have a baby. Even though I had sex with others in the past, Noah was different. I felt like I had given up my innocence for this man. But now my problems had just begun, since I had no way to let him know about the baby. I couldn't write him since my father would find out at the same time. So I didn't tell anyone, and then I didn't have to tell anyone because it became apparent, and I could no longer hide it from anyone. This is far from acceptable to the Amish,- an unmarried woman having a baby. Well needless to say, no one was bubbling over with excitement for me. I really needed to talk to Noah, but I began to wonder if I would ever have any communication with him again. It was very difficult. At this point I was really scared. Would I just have to marry someone? Would they shun me for the rest of my life? I wasn't sure what was going to happen next in my life.

After the first few months, I heard through some of my relatives in the community that Noah had left the Amish and was living on the outside. Well at the time I didn't know what to think about this. I thought that by now he would have surely heard that I was expecting. I had gotten word about his leaving the Amish, so naturally I assumed that he had gotten word about my situation. I dismissed any negative thoughts, and I did not want to believe that possibly he had heard about the baby and decided to skip out all together. I convinced myself that he just did not know I was going to have a baby. I made it my business to find out all I could about where he was and did finally manage to get word to him that I was expecting. Then I began to plan my escape. It took a good deal of planning and scheming, but I arranged to meet Noah on the outside on a particular day at a specified time. My ten year old brother drove me to the rendezvous. I was excited beyond description and frightened at the same time. My dream was coming true, the "outside" was finally going to be a reality.

My heart sank; Noah wasn't there. Again, I dismissed this incident. Looking back now, I guess I should have seen how irresponsible he was. I chose to overlook all of the signs.

Four hours later, he showed up. I was relieved, but the next glaring indication of irresponsibility was when he announced that he was broke. He didn't have any gasoline in his car. I had to give him all the money I had which was only $40.00. This was the beginning of our life together. I can see now how the relationship began with a meager commitment, no money, and a baby on the way. The writing was on the wall, and I was not able to read any of the signs. I wasn't taught to assess situations, I was taught to survive, and to survive with bare minimum requirements.

At this point, we were at the mercy of our family members who lived on the "outside". I had two brothers who were settled into their new life. They were able to help Noah get a job. We got a place to live, though we still weren't married, but within a couple of months we did take the big step. It was rough going at first. We just barely made it before the baby was born. At first everything seemed good, but I was experiencing an entirely different world, a new adventure every day. I actually had some of the modern conveniences that made life so much easier to cope with. Work did not seem as hard with electricity and indoor plumbing. It was all so wonderful. I finally was living my dream, and it was incredible.

Our baby girl was born shortly after we were settled. Unfortunately, when you leave the Amish community, they refuse to acknowledge your existence. I couldn't call my parents and share the good news with them. They had a beautiful granddaughter. But I was an outcast. Even my closest family members were very judgmental toward me. They knew I was on my way to hell, but I just knew I was in heaven. For those who choose to leave, in some cases, it is as if you are dead. I did have some communication with my family. They exhausted themselves trying to get me to come back. But I was not going anywhere because I liked living in the world.

It doesn't take a great deal of material wealth to satisfy some-one who has lived with just the bare-basic necessities of life. When we started earning a decent salary, we considered ourselves to be quite wealthy. We lived a relatively comfortable lifestyle. We were able to buy a home and a car, and this lifestyle was indescribably different from what I was used to growing up. I will say that I missed communicating with my family. It was good to have three of my brothers close. Amish people put a tremendous emphasis on family, and my family was very important to me.

Noah had begun to enjoy the freedom which came with his new found lifestyle. He was full of insults slanted toward the Amish people and their beliefs. He had made drastic changes in his person-ality. He was a real party person now. He jumped right into all that the "outside" had to offer, good or bad. He was so wrapped up in all the world had to offer him, he seemingly forgot he had a family. He rarely came home. As a matter of fact, I rarely saw him. I suspected that he had someone else. I never could prove it, but my instinctive feelings were very strong. Our marriage was on very shaky ground. Our communication was close to nil. It seemed that all we did was fight over how much he was gone. During all of the changes we were encountering in our life, we added two more children to our family. Eight years after the birth of our first child, we had a set of twins. Now there was twice as much work to be done around the house. The birth of these children didn't seem to have any effect on Noah's behavior. He continued right along with his partying and avoided coming home as much as possible. So his lack of concern for his family weighed heavy on me. My feelings for him were dwindling. We lived like this for quite some time. We stayed married mainly because of the children. It was an unspoken understanding between the two of us. I am sure it had a great deal to do with our Amish roots and the traditions that were ingrained in us.

We had been on the "outside" for almost thirteen years when Noah received word that his grandfather had died. He decided he would attend the funeral, and he did. Something happened to Noah while he was at the funeral. He was not the same person when he returned. I don't know if it was something that someone said to him or if it was the actual death of his grandfather, but he had a yearning to return to the Amish community. He did not want to go alone; he wanted to take us all back. This hit me like a ton of bricks. I didn't know what to say. My heart was saying, no way, but my head was saying, "What will you do to provide for these three children?" I couldn't come up with a solid answer. I tried to talk him out of it, but back to the Amish way, the woman does not have anything to say about decisions. The man is the head of the house, and he makes all of the decisions. I felt like I had no other choice but to give in and go. The only reason I did agree to go was for the sake of the children. In reality our marriage was over. We just stayed together because of the children. But everything always points back to those Amish laws we were indoctrinated with since the beginning of our lives.

Another fear I had was that our children didn't know anything about the Amish way of life. They didn't know life without electricity, running water, and so many other luxuries we enjoyed. Noah enticed the oldest child with the promise of owning her own horses. She was ready to go now. Her own horse, WOW!

I was sad and overwhelmed with mixed emotions. I did not want to return. There was no comparison with the life I had to the life I was going back to. Noah promised to take us to a community that offered some amenities, like running water. It was settled that we would return.

Upon our arrival back into the same community we had left some thirteen years earlier, the first thing we had to deal with was changing our clothes. They had Amish clothes waiting for us when we arrived. They even went so far as to tell us we could use our English clothes to make quilts. This was just the beginning. I had truly forgotten how different it was, and there was so much adjusting to do. At first, it was an adventure for the children, especially our oldest, but it soon became a miserable existence for her as well as for me. We were put in the ban at first.

Rejoining the community did not have much impact on Noah, for he was not treated with the same animosity as me and the children. He was treated as the prodigal son, and I was the wayward wife. He continued to stay away from home as much as possible. He found so many people to visit, and he had so much to talk about with everyone. He was reconciling with his roots. I spent most of my time in solitude and had the burden of tending to all of the responsibilities. Needless to say, I felt as though I was going to lose my mind. Of course, we had to repent of the error of our ways. We were made to kneel before the congregation and ask to be forgiven for the wrongs they said we had done. In my mind, I had done nothing wrong. In spite of our rocky marriage, I had found some peace on the outside. We suffered through the ban. They kept all eyes on me, and I knew they were just waiting to catch me at something to reprimand me for, but I was good at following their rules. Still I had not known this kind of suffering before. Before I left, I had not known what I was missing, but now I knew what I had and now what I had to do without. But somehow, I managed to suffer through it all.

Noah announced he had a cousin who was going to come and live with us for awhile. His name was Sam. He was a younger, single man. Sam turned out to be quite a help to me. He was always there, and I was beginning to enjoy having someone around to talk to. I welcomed his offer to help with the twins and other chores that were at hand. Sam and I were together so much, our relationship developed into one that was more than mere friendship. Sam would make me feel good about myself on those days when nothing looked good, especially me. Well, one thing led to another, and before you know it, we were sleeping together. I don't think Noah was aware of what was going on, and if he was, he didn't show any sign of jealousy. I don't think anyone was the wiser. Sam was very curious about what life was like on the "outside". I told him there was no comparison, and I longed to return to the life I had on the "outside".

After about eight months of living in the Amish community, our daughter announced to me how ready she was to go back to "our way of life". She did not consider the Amish lifestyle her way of doing things. She was a complete stranger to the Amish. She had said all I needed to hear. Her desire to escape gave me all the strength I needed to make preparations to leave.

I shared with Sam what my plans were and he agreed to help. He had arranged for a car to be stashed for the day of our getaway. It would be Easter Sunday when we would make our escape. Sam decided that he wanted to go with us. He wanted to try life on the "outside". He said that he loved me and that we could start a new life together. It sounded pretty good at the time, so I agreed.

On Easter Sunday morning, Noah decided to go to another church where one of his cousins was going to preach. This certainly made everything easier for us to make our getaway. When he left for church, we made our way to the car and we were on our way. I had taken half of the money that was in the bank and made arrangements to go to my brother's house. I didn't take much more than those clothes we had worn back to rejoin the community eight months prior.

It didn't take Noah long to set out in search of us. Of course he would come to my brother's house looking for us first. He barged in and demanded that I give him the children. I would not allow him to take them. Our daughter did not want to go back. She vocalized her feelings. She was crying. It was not a pretty scene. My brother insisted that Noah leave and asked him not to come back. This was only the first of our encounters.

I had gotten a job in a restaurant as a waitress and Sam kept the children at first while I worked. I was a bit concerned that Noah would try to take the children while I was working. He made several visits to our house in an effort to persuade the children to return with him. They did not want to go back. Chris, our son, was the only child who expressed a desire to see his dad. The girls didn't seem interested. I never knew when he would show up, so life didn't offer much peace during those days. One night in particular, he came, and as usual when he got there, he urged the children to return with him. As usual, Chris was the only one who would greet him with a hug and kiss. It was then that Noah grabbed him and took off to a van that was waiting outside.

I couldn't believe what was happening. All I knew to do was call the police and tell them what happened. There wasn't much they could do since we were still married, and Chris was his child. They suggested that I contact an attorney at this point. The very first thing the next day, I called an attorney. After I had explained everything to her, she said since we were still married, there wasn't much I could do legally. So I began to consider what options I had and just exactly what I should do next.

I decided that the only way I was going to get my son back was to go take him much the same way Noah had taken him. So after much thought, I laid the plans for getting him home. I asked my brother to drive me to the community late one night. My daughter went with me to help get her brother back. We waited until it was very late at night. My brother parked the car about a mile from the house where we used to live. This way no one would be aware of our approach.

I walked for a mile in the dark through the tree-lined lane with no more than the light of the moon and stars to guide me. The walk seemed to drag on and on as I became more and more nervous that I would be detected. "What if the dogs begin to bark?" I worried. The dogs, though, did not pay any attention to me.

As I approached the house, it was totally dark and there didn't appear to be any life stirring inside. So I walked right up to the front door, and at this point, my heart was beating uncontrollably. As I opened the door, I held my breath hoping the hinges on the door wouldn't squeak as I entered the house. Stopping to listen, I decided that it was okay to proceed. Just as I entered the living room, I noticed that Noah was asleep on the couch. My heart leaped up into my throat, and I momentarily forgot to breathe. Noah did not move, and I realized that I was safe to continue on. Walking past my husband, I went to a desk in order to retrieve a flashlight that I knew to be in the top drawer. I again walked past Noah, watching to see if he would wake up. He remained asleep, and I waited till I was in the hallway that led to my son's room before I turned on the flashlight.

Walking straight into the bedroom I noticed there were three boys sleeping in the same bed. By this point my heart felt like it was going to burst from my chest, but I had to keep my wits together since

I was so close to getting my son out of the house. In order for me to know which boy was Chris, I shined the flashlight at the base of the bed and gradually moved it up until I knew where he was. There was my son in the middle. I turned off the flashlight and reached over to pick him up. With my heart pounding in my ear, I scooped up Chris and placed him on my shoulder, all the while making sure that I did not wake the other two boys. So that we would not have to walk past Noah, I carried Chris through the kitchen and out the back door. Not one person in the house had even the slightest notion that we were there.

All the while, I was so frightened. I kept looking back over my shoulder waiting for someone to come after me. My fear prodded me to walk faster and faster, and at about this time, Chris woke up and said to me, "I will keep an eye out for Daddy." Again, I feared that the dogs would bark at us as we left, but they never made a sound. Down the lane I went with Chris in my arms, almost running now. We made it back to the car, jumped in, and locked the door quickly behind us. As the car took off for home, I heaved a sigh of relief and tried to calm my shaking hands. No one was the wiser until the next morning.

The very next day, I filed for divorce and requested that I be given sole custody of our three children. This was the only weapon I had to fight with to prevent Noah from coming again and trying to take my son away. After filing for the divorce, I just waited for Noah to show up again. I knew he would.

Two weeks later, Noah was back. He was very nice and never mentioned the divorce. I suspected that he had already received the papers. Something prompted this unexpected visit. He very politely and humbly asked to see the children. The girls did not want to see him, but our son was eager to see him. I never suspected he would try anything again. Especially with the legal document I had which was intended to prevent him from taking the children, surely he would not repeat any of the prior events. I went so far as to ask him if he was going to try anything, and he assured me that he just wanted to see the children. I believed him. But he had said only what I wanted to hear, and he pulled the same stunt again. My heart sank and panic swept over me. This time I did have a leg to stand on, and the very next morning, I phoned my attorney. This time I had legal grounds to get my son back. I decided it would be best to let the law handle his return this time. I certainly did not want to do anything that would weaken my case in the courtroom. This time though, Noah had sent the child out of town. It took the law just a little longer than I anticipated. It was close to a month before I finally got the call telling me they had picked Noah up, and I could come down and get my son. I was so relieved to have my son back. Chris was drained. He felt like a pawn in a game. He loved his father, but he did not understand what was motivating his actions. He decided that he was tired of playing these games, and this would be the last time he would be used as a pawn.

The divorce was final. I was awarded total custody of the children and child support in the amount of $150.00 a month. When Noah received the notice, he didn't waste any time before paying us another visit.

Well this time was not like the others. No one wanted to go see Daddy. But he was persistent and finally our son did agree to talk to him, but he refused to get close enough to touch. He wasn't going to fall for the same trick again. Noah didn't realize what harm this was doing to their relationship. The harm could not be seen, only felt within the heart and soul of his son. Noah couldn't see the wall he was building between himself and the children. They were beginning to resent their dad. It was a real issue with our oldest daughter. She could see right through him. She was harboring a very bitter attitude toward him. I tried very hard not to add any fuel to the fire by making unkind remarks about Noah to the children. It was not always an easy thing to do.

After the dust had all settled and the commotion died down, it was time now to look at the situation with Sam. The reality was that I hadn't had much time to concern myself with Sam, who, by the way, was still living with us. One important thing had occurred to me: I was not interested in settling for someone to be with, to share the responsibilities with just for the sake of having someone around. I was much better off in every way, if all I had to concern myself with was myself and my children. That was more than enough. So Sam and I parted ways before everything got blown out of proportion and I had another ordeal to cope with.

I really didn't know what life held for me. I thought I had

experienced more than enough heartache in my marriage. All I was concerned about at this point was providing for myself and my children. My brothers offered so much support to us, financially and emotionally. They were there for me when I needed them. I don't know what would have happened to us if it weren't for them.

The task at hand for me was to find a job. For a woman with only an eighth grade education, there are not a lot of opportunities, and where there was work, the pay was not adequate. Fortunately, I was very well trained in every area concerning domestic issues. I could bake anything. So with that in mind, my brother offered to set me up in a bakery business. All went well in the beginning. The business required all of my time and attention. The children helped when they weren't in school, but it required such long hours, and after awhile, we all decided it would be best to sell out. Once again, I was searching for just the right job. In between jobs, my brothers were always there to lend a hand. In just a short while, I was able to find a job with the local university, cooking and baking for one of their sororities. This job has truly been a blessing to me. I can use my talents cooking to provide a living, and I enjoy caring for the children. It has been good for me all the way around. So far, we have not been without anything. It has required hard work and all of my strength, but if I could change anything, I still would not return to the Amish.

Noah has yet to send the first child support payment. Several attempts have been made by my attorney to get him into court. But he has been hiding behind the Amish community and their doctrines. He contends that he is not subject to the English laws; after all he is Amish. He has been successful in obtaining support from the National Old Order Amish Steering Committee. The courts have received letters from numerous bishops. Noah would receive up to 70 letters or more a week from his fellow Amish supporters.

Noah would show up from time to time and try to convince the children to return with him. His scare tactics had no effect on them because they knew the truth. Noah, on the other hand, denied the fact that we were even divorced. According to his beliefs, we would be married forever. But he didn't feel any remorse for not supporting his children. I could not find an ounce of compassion for him. He had lived on both sides of the fence. If he were such a good Christian, how could he refuse to support his own flesh and blood?

The Amish do not accept divorce. Noah bases his entire case around the Amish beliefs and doctrines. I often thought if we had not returned to the Amish community, we would still be married today. I contend that despite Noah's beliefs regarding our marriage or our divorce, he is responsible for providing for the children. My argument is that if he feels so strongly about his faith, then surely he knows what God says about a man providing for his family. Of course he disagrees with me. The truth of the matter is that Noah is a very selfish man. How could he expect these children to turn away from what they had grown up with and convert to such a backward lifestyle? It is one thing when you don't know what it is like to live on the outside, but when the opposite is true, it is a totally different story.

Before I was Amish, I was a human being. I only joined the Amish religion because I did not have any other choice. It goes without saying when you are born, you will join the church. It is expected of you. Everything in your life revolves around the Amish doctrine and the Amish way. I was taught as far back as I can remember that everyone outside the Amish will surely go to hell. If you never hear anything to contradict that or are never allowed to explore other options, you will grow up believing exactly what was drilled into your head.

After having lived on the "outside" for such a long time, I have discovered that many people from other countries outside the United States dream of becoming an American citizen. Their dreams are motivated by the fact that America is the land of the free, and there is such opportunity for everyone to succeed. Being Amish, I was born in the United States, and yet I did not experience this freedom, and if I dared to try it, I was condemned and severely punished. It is easily compared to a prison system within the United States. Amish set themselves apart from some of the governing rules, such as social security. That is they do not pay into the social security system, but now they do pay federal income tax. But oddly enough, they participate in any program that offers them something for free. They seek these programs out and want to take full advantage of them, but that is all they want from the government. In everything else, they stand on the laws governing separation between church and state. This is very difficult for me to swallow.

Noah uses his Amish heritage as an excuse to dodge paying child support. A man who professes to believe that marriage is sacred and a life long commitment refuses to support the children of this sacred relationship. To date, the law has not been successful in forcing him to pay or suffer the consequences. They were successful in lodging him in a local jail for a short period of time. But the issue of the back child support is still a very real issue since he owes over $50,000. This money would provide a college education for the twins. He says in his eyes we are still married, and yet refuses to assume his role as the head of the house and support his family. While he lived on the outside for thirteen years and enjoyed his life of freedom in the United States, all three of his children were born outside of the Amish community. They were his children then, and they are still his children. If anyone should suffer the consequences, shouldn't it be him? Not the innocent children. How can the Amish stand behind a man who has for all intents and purposes turned his back on his own flesh and blood? These innocent children are the victims in this case. How can the Amish allow this man to hide behind them in order to ignore his responsibility? What difference does it make that nowhere in the history of the Amish has anyone ever broken from the community, taken custody of the children, and then demanded child support in a lawsuit? They failed to mention that Noah fled the Amish community for some thirteen years, during which time he was married and had all three of these children. Also, during that thirteen years, lived on the wild side with all of his partying, drinking, and the like. Their failure to acknowledge the whole truth clearly illuminates the glaring truth about who they are and what they stand for, just whatever suits them for the time being. These innocent children have only known one lifestyle, and it consisted of running water, electricity, and automobiles, and the list goes on. Most people in the United States take all of these things for granted. The Amish believe that all of these things are sinful and go directly against the word of God. So even though this was the only lifestyle they were used to, they were taken into the Amish community. What they had to put up with during those eight months was like prison to them. They could not be brainwashed to believe what the Amish believe. They had experienced first hand all of the things that the Amish said were sinful. The life they had known was not a sinful life.

70

They had a good life outside of the Amish. They had grown up under the laws that govern the citizens of the United States. Electricity, running water, and the entire modern day lifestyle are not wrong, quite the contrary because they are intended for our use to enjoy. God gave us life as a gift. He created all of us, and to each one of us He gave gifts and talents. The people down through the ages who invented and discovered all of the technology have not committed sin by doing so, but quite the opposite, they have used their God given talents to be the very best they could be. It wasn't by chance that electricity was discovered, rather it was part of God's plan. The conveniences of life do not make us sinful since it is in his weakness that man chooses to sin.

When Noah took these children back into a community that provided security for him, they were strangers to the entire community. Their life was completely turned upside down. Control and condemnation was all around them. Of course women don't have any say so in the Amish community, so my hands were tied. When I agreed to go back with Noah, I thought I was doing the right thing to keep the family together. I had no idea what impact this would have on the children. My children were being subjected to all of the mental abuse and what I believe is the same tactic as brain washing while living amongst the Amish. I did not want them to suffer the same abuse that I had suffered as a child. I wanted more for them.

Noah contends that I have no place on the "outside" and since I was born Amish, I would always be Amish. He could not see past what he wanted for himself to understand how this abrupt lifestyle change affected his children. Noah was always raised to believe that the man has the say-so, and you do not dispute what he says or does. I believe the man should be the head of the house, but Noah did not take on that role with our family, inside the Amish community or outside. He chose to stay away as much as possible, and I was the one who was left to make decisions regarding day to day living and so on. Consequently, the children never saw him as the head of our house. They saw a man who liked to drink, party, and carouse.

I have had to struggle to obtain the basic necessities for the children and me. I have had to work long hard hours much the same as when I was Amish. I don't mind the hard work. The major difference is that we have not had to live under the strife and condemnation that would come with living under the Amish rule. The eight months that the children and I rejoined the Amish was living hell for us. We may not have a great deal of money, but we have peace of mind when we lay our heads down at night. The children don't want to have anything to do with their dad. He will only acknowledge them if they return to the Amish community. Otherwise it is as if they don't exist. This is one of the biggest fallacies within the Amish community: they deny their own flesh and blood.

I believe that I have learned more about God and the life He created than I ever would have if I had remained in the Amish community. I have been blessed to see my children grow up and have a full understanding of what life is all about. They have experienced the joy and the sorrows of being raised by a single parent, but they have seen more real love than I ever saw in my life time being raised with my entire family. I believe that we are all stronger because of the struggles we have survived. My children and I have a bond that cannot be broken by any doctrine or law. I thank God that I can honestly say I forgive Noah, because I believe that he does not truly know what he is doing.

Chapter Seven
George and Lydia

From the time he was a small boy George Yoder knew that he wanted to be a carpenter. While most Amish boys grow up to be farmers, George wanted to take a different path. Nothing felt better to George than sawing, hammering, and sanding wood into elegant cabinets, barns, and houses. The smell of pine or oak was more appealing to him than the smell of manure and earth. Just as George enjoyed the hard work of building barns and the delicate concentration of building cabinets, he looked to build his inner self on a strong foundation that was based on God.

. In 1952, George was born to Enos E. Yoder and Elizabeth Yoder in the community of Bowling Green, Missouri. Eventually this family grew to include four daughters and six sons. Life for George and his family was happy, though they did not have much. A misconception sometimes made about the Amish is that everyone in the community is provided for on an equal scale. This is not so, for each Amish family is responsible for providing for its own needs. In the case of George's family they worked hard, but they never had much money. Nevertheless, the children's needs were always met.

At an early age George began working on his father's farm. Like the adults, the children were required to work in the fields, doing the same work the adults did including plowing. George was different though because of his strong desire to be a carpenter. With determination swelling up inside him, George began looking for ways to learn the art of carpentry. When he was eight years old, George began sneaking nails from his father's supply so he could practice hammering them into old boards. This small beginning had George hooked, and he knew that he needed to do more than just practice his hammering; instead George needed to continue his education in carpentry. To learn more, George would linger around his grandfather who would do little fix-it jobs. He would watch as his grandfather carefully measured and cut the wood for whatever project he was working on. Though his grandfather could do small jobs, George wanted to learn more about building larger structures. From the wise grandfather, George went to his uncle who was a carpenter and a farmer. At first George just watched as his uncle practiced the craft of carpentry. Eventually George assisted his uncle in building such things as barns, toolsheds, and houses.

All this studying and careful observation paid off for George when one day his mother made the comment that she would like a new chicken house. Without saying a word, George went out to the yard and chose a nice spot for the new chicken house. Next he chose the wood to be used, wanting solid boards of wood that could withstand the elements of nature. Taking pride in his work, George measured, sawed, and hammered a fine structure for his mother's hens. This was accomplished when George was only eleven years old. The very next year George built his father a machine shed with a concrete footer. Though he was just twelve, George had the insight to be as thorough as any adult would have been. These first two structures were just the beginning for George and his love of carpentry.

* * *

George strove to be a good Amish child, and he listened to what his elders said about getting into heaven. The ideas that George took from his elders dealt with his worth as a child of God. Even as young as eight years old George worried about being worthy enough for heaven. His concern grew so that at night when everything was quiet, George would pray to God that if his soul at that moment was clean, would God please take him at that moment so that he could go to heaven. Fear about heaven and hell constantly crept into George's thoughts when he was a child.

One day when George was in the first grade at Woodlawn Country School, his teacher had the class put up their text books as usual. All the children busied themselves in putting away their various books and straightening up their desks. Nothing seemed out of the ordinary to George on this particular day. The teacher, when she saw that the class was ready, said, "Everybody rise." When all the children had risen, George thought he heard his teacher say, "Jesus is coming tonight." Being the young child that he was, George was frightened by this statement. He was not sure that he was ready for Jesus to come as is predicted in the Bible. So from school, George went home and asked his mother about what the teacher had said. His mother tried to comfort him and tell him that no one knows when Jesus was to come back to earth. But George was afraid that what the teacher said would come true, so he set a day and a time when he would begin behaving perfectly, which included not fighting with his brothers and obeying his parents. Only later did George learn that what his teacher really said was, "Suppose Jesus is coming." Years later, this incident came to symbolize for George the fear that is placed in the Amish children by the Amish ministers, bishops, and parents.

By the time George Yoder became a teenager, the fear tactics of the Amish began to wear off. The type of friends that George associated with were considered to be a bit wild; and like many of his peers, George smoked and even did some minor drinking. His friends were Andy and Sam Schwartz, Dave Mast, and Albert Mast. These boys developed a reputation for being trouble makers and soon George was looked down upon for hanging out with them.

Not long after he began fraternizing with the Schwartz boys, George got into trouble with the church. The whole affair stemmed from a radio. In the Amish religion, modern conveniences are considered worldly and therefore evil. This line of thinking extended to the radio. The boys knew that if they were to get caught they would receive a punishment, so they decided to devise a story to cover their tracks. Each boy knew what he was to say but despite the lie they created, someone in the church discovered the radio. Since George knew about the radio, he was considered as bad as the Swartz boys even though he did not own the radio and he was not caught using the radio. As a result, George was excommunicated from the church for four weeks. This meant that he had to receive his meals at a table that was placed to one side of the kitchen, and he could not have any contact with anyone other than his family. Though his parents were disappointed in him, they never stopped being kind to George. Neither of his parents really talked about the situation with George despite the fact that it was an extremely embarrassing situation. One day, George's grandfather George commented as George, Levi Yoder and his brother were passing by, "Stay away from these boys." Besides that one comment, nothing was ever said to George about the radio incident.

Enos Yoder always tried to support his son no matter what George did. Therefore, when George got the idea to start his own shop so that he could do carpentry work, his father helped him begin this new venture. Material, money, and a few basic machines were all furnished by Enos so that George could try to launch his carpentry business. George built his own shop and began making such things as desks. Not only did George build for his uncle, but also he built things for the Amish in his community. On occasion George would hear people say, "Oh there's no way you can make a business of this. Many people have tried it and nobody's been successful." Though these words were bitter to hear, George continued on because of his determination. Eventually things were going well for him, and by the age of twenty George was able to pay back what he owed his father. Because of the Amish tradition, George had to continue to give his father the earnings from the carpentry shop even after the debt had been cleared. Most of the time the father keeps the wages of his children until they reach the age of twenty-one. But in George's case, he was able to start keeping his wages once he was twenty and a half. Why George was able to begin keeping his money six months earlier stemmed from the fact that when his older brother was twenty and a half he was allowed to keep his own earnings because he had just been married. Since the older brother was able to do this, George was allowed to begin six months early as well.

* * *

While the fear that the Amish had put into him when he was a child had worn off by the time George entered the church at age seventeen, still he was looking for reassurance from God. What seemed to be a series of close calls might actually have been signals from God that George needed to wake up and realize that it was God who should be turned to and not a list of ordinances. These close calls might have been what George needed to see that God was with him and would not forsake him.

The first close call happened when George ran into Levi one afternoon. These two youths were wrestling around in a barn, when George lost his balance and fell behind the horse. The horse startled and kicked. One hoof grazed George's eyebrow, and if George's head had been a fraction of an inch higher in the air, then George probably would have been killed.

Another incident happened when George and Levi were tearing down an old house. Both George and Levi were working when, without warning part, of the roof fell and knocked George down. A nail that had been in the roof hit him in the center of his nose. Fortunately George was not seriously hurt, but he could have been if the nail had hit him a half inch on either side of his nose.

A third close call occurred when George was riding along in a car with a customer who wanted George to measure for some cabinets. As the two men were waiting to turn left, a gravel truck hit them from behind, which thrust the vehicle into the oncoming traffic lane. George narrowly escaped being hit by oncoming traffic.

Because of the various accidents, George began to wonder if God was preparing him for something bigger. But for George to be ready, he needed to be more aware of his life and what was going on in it. These few incidents may have allowed George to open his mind for the message God wanted him to hear. Though these occurrences began when he was seventeen, he was twenty-eight before George knew exactly what God intended for him.

* * *

Once George Yoder turned seventeen, he began to date, and like many seventeen year old boys, George was a bit fickle, but George may have been more fickle than the average person. From the ages of seventeen to twenty George dated between thirty to thirty-five girls.

One day George met Lydia S. Troyer who was the daughter of Sam S. and Elizabeth Troyer. Lydia had been born in Indiana and moved around with her family from Tennessee and Pennsylvania. It was when Lydia came to Bowling Green that she and George met. After dating seven or eight months, George and Lydia married and began establishing their home. With a work shop already built, George began work on his and Lydia's house. As soon as the house was completed, different members of the church began to complain that George and Lydia's house looked too worldly. Neighbors said that the windows were too close together and should be separated more. Also the neighbors complained that George and Lydia had an indoor bathroom. In reality, George had not built the outhouse yet. Not only did neighbors complain about the outside of the house, but when they would come over for visits they would complain that the woodwork was stained and that there were outside corners with no woodwork. These things were prohibited by the Amish church.

After awhile George began construction on a new work shop, but instead of building the traditional shop, he wanted to try a new style as a means of challenging himself. Like the house he built, the new shop caused much complaining among the people of the Amish community. Certain members of the church complained because they could not see the siding between the windows when the shop was viewed from the road; and they complained that the front door had glass knobs. As a result, George painted the glass knobs in order to make them look more plain. Also, members of the community complained that the side doors appeared to be too much like a garage door. These changes from the traditional style were classified as too worldly and not of the Amish way. Because of all the complaints, George decided to sell his shop as a way of relieving some of the pressure he was feeling from the community.

George was not the only one who was feeling the pressure of the community. George's wife Lydia was receiving complaints because of her style of dress. Coming from a different settlement was difficult because there were different rules. Lydia did not like the people in Missouri because they would continually complain that her dress and cap were not as they should be. One day after church a group of ministers called Lydia to them and criticized her so much that she began to cry. When George saw what they were doing to her, he marched over to his wife and told the ministers to leave her alone. With pressure on the both of them, George and Lydia decided to move to Snyder, Pennsylvania. George's parents were getting ready to move to Tennessee so there was no real reason to stay. Once in Pennsylvania, life was much happier for the couple who already had two children, George, Jr. and Andrew. Just as he had done in Bowling Green, George built a shop and began his carpentry business again. In Snyder, George was able to conduct more business with non-Amish customers, or as the Amish would call them the English.

* * *

Before George and Lydia left Bowling Green, Missouri, George had the opportunity to become friends with Carl Hasty who was a deputy policeman. The first time Carl stopped by George's shop, George noticed that Carl had a copy of the Bible on the dashboard of his police car. George thought this strange since he believed the Bible preached non-violence. One day while talking with Carl, the subject of the Bible came up. Carl wanted to know why George dressed the way he did and George responded that he believed the Bible told him to dress as he was. In an attempt to explain that George was misguided, Carl said that in the end clothes did not determine whether a person reached heaven or not. Unfortunately, George did not understand what Carl was saying to him, especially since George believed the only true Bible was the German version used by the Amish. While George was not ready to hear what Carl was saying to him, the conversation stayed in the back of his mind and acted as a means of opening his mind to the true message of God.

George's time to listen to God's message came two years after he and his wife had moved to Pennsylvania. George and Lydia were in Missouri visiting George's brother-in-law, Ben Girod. Ben mentioned to George that going to heaven is not like a shot in the dark, rather one must accept Jesus Christ as being the Savior. In seeing how Ben accepted Jesus as his Savior, George thought that he, too, was ready to do the same thing. It was on this trip that George began reading an English Bible.

Once George and Lydia returned to Pennsylvania, George began seeking out Bible study meetings. His actions greatly upset Lydia's family, and they began to collect information on what George was doing. Lydia's family wanted to know if what George was doing greatly conflicted with what the Amish church was teaching. The

Amish began pushing George and Lydia out of the community. This left George and Lydia to attend the Mennonite church. Eventually Lydia's father, who was a bishop, decided that both George and Lydia should be excommunicated from the Amish church.

During the last year before George and Lydia left the Amish, Lydia had a hard time determining whether or not she wanted to leave the church. Her family kept pressuring her to remain in the church and to leave George. Lydia could not even talk to the English people who would come over to have Bible study with George. Eventually Lydia began talking to the wife of a local pastor, especially about how one becomes saved. The pastor's wife reassured Lydia that in accepting Christ as the Savior, Lydia would be saved by God's grace. After contemplating all that was said to her, Lydia decided that she would give up the Amish religion and accept Christ as her Savior. Once Lydia made this decision, both she and George walked completely away from their Amish tradition.

* * *

A new life was ahead for George and Lydia, but they never would have expected that their life would change because of a conference that was being held in Delaware. While at the conference, George learned about a college that was in Crown Point, Indiana called Hyles Anderson College. After some consideration, George decided that he would move his family to Indiana so that he could attend this college. Times were tough for George and his family, but he made ends meet by building cabinets for a shop in Gary, Indiana and by being the shop teacher at Hamond Baptist High School. Though he was having to juggle school and two jobs, George was happy living the English life. At the end of five years, George only had thirty credits left, but he had to finish those credits by going to night school. After another year of school, George graduated with a bachelor of science in pastoral theology. Though he has his college degree, George still teaches shop at Hamond Baptist High School to kids in grades nine through twelve.

Though life for George and his family has been happy since leaving the Amish church, it has not been without some sadness. Because they have been excommunicated, they are shunned by many of their different family members. A few members will still speak to them, like Lydia's parents. But though her parents will speak to them, they are not always so accepting of the new lifestyle George has chosen for his family. As for George's parents, they have never admonished him for his leaving, but he knows that they are disappointed in his decision to leave. But George knew that he had to leave the Amish faith because of the inconsistencies. For example, George had a conversation with his father-in-law about modern inventions. George simply pointed out that the wheelbarrow that his father-in-law was using was at one time a modern invention, just as the horse and buggy and car. The father-in-law did not want to think of the car as being in the same category as the horse and buggy. George pointed out that the father-in-law had ridden in vehicles before, but all the father-in-law could reply was, "You know how it is."

The hypocrisy of the Amish religion is the biggest reason that George would never consider returning to the Amish. In all the years that George was Amish, he saw his fellow Amish use the modern conveniences of the English neighbors, yet the Amish bishops would say that owning anything modern would be sinful. Many times George did wonder why this was the case when it did not make any sense. In George's own life, he had a shop that was deemed too worldly by the Amish community in which he lived. Because of the pressure, George sold his shop and moved. One of George's biggest critics later built a shop that was even larger than George's. To George, the action of the bishop was the greatest hypocrisy that he had ever witnessed. Hypocrisy such as this drove George away.

While George does not like the fear tactics of the Amish and their insistence that modern conveniences are evil, he does still acknowledge that the Amish do have good qualities. These good qualities include having a good work ethic, teaching honesty, and instilling character into the children. Remembering these good qualities keeps George and his wife from having any bitter feelings towards the Amish. They are happy to just live as they choose and to raise their six children.

For George, leaving the Amish was difficult, but he knew that he had to in order to fulfill his dreams of being a carpenter and a good Christian. If he had stayed with the Amish, George would have been controlled and kept ignorant of the truth about God and about the

Bible. George was lucky, though, because he had people in his life who made him open his eyes and examine what the Amish were doing to their followers. Along with Carl Hastings, George is grateful to Ura Yoder who, as George says, was greatly responsible for making him take an honest look at his life. Others, too, have been helpful in influencing George, such as his close friends Levi and Glen Yoder. These people supported George and his family as they made the transition from Amish to English and fortunately for George and his family, they can now live in peace and harmony.

Chapter Eight
Joe and Rachel

The story of Joe and Rachel Schrock is about truth. While with the Amish, Joe and Rachel felt that they were not being instructed on how a good person should live according to the standards set up by God, rather they felt that they were being instructed on how to live according to rules set forth by man. Because of their doubts, these two honest and caring people set out to find for themselves what God really wanted them to do with their lives. In looking for answers, Joe and Rachel discovered that they had to leave the Amish faith so that they could have the freedom to live according to God's standards and not man's. This decision was difficult, for in leaving the Amish, the Schrocks would put in jeopardy their relationship with their Amish relatives. This story of the Schrocks is about their exodus from the limiting Amish lifestyle to the freedom of their English life.

* * *

Joe Mose Schrock, son of Mose J. Schrock and Wilma Yoder Schrock, was born in 1944 in Portland, Indiana. Until he became a member of the Amish church at the age of seventeen, Joe was considered a follower. As a follower, Joe would go to church every Sunday and would be instructed as to what he must do to become a member of the church and as to how a good Amish member lives. In order to maintain a "good standing" with the Amish church and community, one had to join the church, be baptized, and become a member of the church between the ages of sixteen and nineteen. Because of this rule, the older adults would place a great amount of pressure upon the young adults to join the Amish faith. Remembering when he was seventeen, Joe says, You automatically feel like you need to make a decision to become a member of the church.

Rachel Schrock was born in Loogootee, Indiana, in 1945 to Dave Eicher and Sarah Marner Eicher. The life she had with her parents and fourteen siblings was usually happy, but there were times when Rachel was confused and unhappy due to what the Amish preachers taught her.

Rachel says, "When I was growing up, probably in my teenage years, the preacher would preach how precious the Bible is and then he'd preach about hell and about how strict we should be not to go there. I always thought how precious the Bible is and the Amish only have church every other Sunday. So, on the in-between Sunday I would always think oh, I bet my dad can't wait to get to the Bible, especially after a good sermon about how good the Bible is. So I thought he never touches it during the week, but then we never did either. So then I thought because they would quote Joshua in the Old Testament about the father teaching whether lying down or sitting up and I'd think I bet he can't wait to read the Bible this morning."

But to Rachel's disappointment her father's Sunday ritual consisted of reading the morning newspapers followed by a family gathering to read a few scriptures from the Bible. Her father was good in explaining the scriptures to the family, but this was the extent to which her father would spend with the Bible. Rachel's disappointment would sometimes lead her to cry quietly in her room. Rachel could not understand why the preachers would talk about the goodness of the Bible in church, yet her father would not involve his family more with the Bible. She tried to read it on her own, but since she and her people spoke a dialect called Pennsylvania Dutch and the Amish Bible is written in German, Rachel only understood the basics of what the text was telling her. She was left to grapple with the message given to her by the preachers and the message that her father's actions set before her.

In looking back on their young adulthood, both Joe and Rachel realized that they were aware of the strictness of the Amish religion, but at that age they did not question the strictness of the Amish faith. As adults, Joe and Rachel saw that the careful attention and strictness towards the children was a result of fear.

Rachel says, "They are concerned about their children staying Amish."

"Yes" Joe agrees, "staying Amish or staying what they call right and doing what we've always done. They don't want their children to make changes. In other words, if dad did it like this and mama did it like this, that's the way the children ought to do it."

* * *

Joe and Rachel met in Bowling Green, Missouri, began dating, and after five years decided that they were ready to enter into marriage. In the Amish culture, the decision to get married must be mutual. For Joe and Rachel this decision was made in the year 1966, but they had to put off their wedding plans for a few years so that Joe could go to the University of Missouri Experimental Farm for the next two years to work so that he could avoid the draft. Because Amish are conscientious objectors, they had to work in hospitals as orderlies or on farms during the draft. The period of time that they had to do this work was two years which is the same amount of time that a soldier would spend for a tour of duty, and the Amish call this period of time the Service. Marrying Joe before he left for the university would have been hard on Rachel because she would not have been able to go with him, and Joe felt that being married and separated from each other would not have been the best thing for them. So Joe went off to the University of Missouri without Rachel. Joe was unsure how to feel about his avoidance of the Vietnam war. He says, "I felt I was inconsistent about that, although I was taught and had it drilled in my mind that you don't go to war or partake of anything like that. I had mixed feelings."

After he returned home to Bowling Green in September of 1968, Joe Schrock and Rachel Eicher married on October 10, 1968. Once married, Joe and Rachel lived in a little shack on a forty acre farm that had been bought before Joe left for the university. As they began life together, everything seemed right, and they were happy with what they had. Joe says, "If there was anybody that needed to be Amish, it was us."

The next ten years of the Schrock family's life went by in happiness. But about the year 1978 or 1979, Joe and Rachel began to have feelings of discontent. During this time, Joe was a member of the school board and he became better acquainted with a man by the name of Glen Yoder who was a school teacher to the Schrock children. Not only did Glen teach the various subjects found in any school, but he also taught scripture to the children. Joe, being extremely open minded, asked Glen Yoder some questions about the Bible. Like Rachel, Joe could not read the German text of the Bible very well. In fact, most of the lay persons in the Amish religion do not read much German so they must rely on the bishop's and minster's interpretations of the Bible. This imbalance of power in Joe and Rachel's case proved to be detrimental, for through the teachings of Glen Yoder, the Schrocks began to understand that the Amish clergy were taking parts of the scripture out of context, and they were misrepresenting what the Bible was teaching.

Going to Glen Yoder was a tremendous step on the part of the Schrocks because the Amish frowned on anyone in their religion asking questions and studying the Bible. But Joe and Rachel needed to turn to someone who could understand the Bible, especially at that time when there was much confusion and contention within the Amish church. Much of the confusion and contention arose from the various rules set forth by the Amish church. Joe and Rachel felt that all the rules were getting in the way of the main focus of the Amish church. Their dissatisfaction led to questions and a concern for the path their children might take as members of the Amish church. So they turned to Glen Yoder, who questioned the Schrocks about the Amish rules. The questioning allowed Joe and Rachel to examine their belief system and its relevance to being a Christian.

Associating with Glen Yoder made the Schrocks stand out among their Amish community. In the beginning, only Joe went to Glen's in order to study and to listen as Glen explained various passages from the Bible. Rachel was not in agreement with Joe's actions because she was afraid of what the Amish would say.

She comments, "I was scared. I didn't want to be different than the Amish."

Joe adds, "You're so conscious of what others think, and when you want to be in good standing with the Amish church, you just think of what people think. It's peer pressure."

Despite the sense that he was going against his religion, Joe continued to meet at the Yoderís farm. These meetings would take place at night as a way to avoid the inquiring eyes of Joe's neighbors.

That Joe was attempting to study the Bible in depth was not the only problem the Amish had with his actions; the fact that he was studying with someone who was using an English Bible caused more problems for Joe. To the strict-thinking Amish, the English are all evil despite the fact that English people go to church and read the Bible. To the Amish, though, the English Bible is not the word of God, instead the Amish see the English Bible as a heresy. Why would the Amish think an English translation of the Bible is a heresy? For the most part, the Amish are afraid that the lay people will see for themselves that the Amish are more about man made rules than the word of God, and that might result in large numbers of members leaving the Amish church. So while the Amish believe that the English are evil, they still use the services that the English provide, like driving Amish groups to a desired location. In fact, the Amish have a saying which goes, "You can use, just don't misuse."

Joe found reading the English Bible to be much easier, and he began to understand more of the Bible. Eventually Joe asked if an English Bible could be obtained for him. Once Joe had the new Bible, Rachel began to read it and began to understand more and more of what the Bible was saying. But though Rachel was reading this English version of the Bible, she still had fears of the Amish discovering that she and Joe were breaking Amish rules. Rachel says, "The preachers would, every service, preach about these strange books and I'm the type when I get cornered like that, I turn red and I was just scared to go to church anymore because they'd end up preaching (about the strange books) and I didn't want to be pointed out."

Though Joe and Rachel tried to keep their actions a secret, their Amish community eventually discovered that they were going outside the church in order to learn about God and the Bible. On one night in particular, Rachel and Joe were on their way to Glen Yoder's. It was a chilly night; Joe and Rachel had the umbrella up, and as they passed another buggy with its umbrella up, the occupants of the other buggy turned around and flashed on Joe and Rachel with a flashlight. The two were preachers, and to Rachel it was as if she and her husband were being hunted and persecuted. Of course the two preachers were observing the direction Joe and Rachel were going; and at that moment, Joe and Rachel knew that they had been discovered, for they were visiting a man who was probably the most hated in that Amish community.

* * *

Because of the Schrock's search for truth, they realized that they needed to move from the Bowling Green, Missouri, settlement. Fortunately, Joe and Rachel heard of Petey Burkholder who was wanting to move and start a new settlement. The appeal to move with Petey Burkholder depended upon many factors. That Petey was a bishop, a relative of Rachel's through marriage, and the same age as the Schrocks helped to persuade Joe and Rachel to move with him. But most importantly, Petey Burkholder was looking for truth.

With the decision to move came the need to search for land. Eventually the group that was moving from Bowling Green, Missouri, decided on land in the Maywood/Philadelphia area which is north of Bowling Green. Once the group had land, they began to discuss what ordinances they would have. The Schrocks, Petey Burkholder, and the other families who would be moving were in agreement that they wanted more liberties, more freedom, than the settlement in Bowling Green allowed. Joe realized that wanting more freedom to use modern conveniences was not an unholy desire. If one of the strictest settlements could use diesel engines, then Joe saw no reason why their new settlement could not use such things as a chain saw or a battery fencer.

When the Schrocks moved to the new settlement in August of 1982, they had not thought about leaving the Amish, just as Petey Burkholder did not intend to leave the Amish church. What they did want was an opportunity to live in a manner that was less strict than what they had been accustomed to. While they agreed to make these changes, Petey Burkholder wanted the changes to come slowly. Burkholder's fear was that if they came out too quickly, then the other Amish in the surrounding communities might attempt to excommunicate them. Joe and Rachel continued to dress as the Amish did, but they did not feel that Petey's suggestion of moving around from one church to another would be of any help to them. At this point, though, Joe and Rachel did not care anymore about the Amish way, and they did not place any importance in what other Amish members thought of them. Joe says, "We had learned enough in the Bible to see that the truth is in God's word, not what people see or think....We had already accepted Christ, and we knew that salvation is in the blood of Christ, not in man's ordinances or in what man thinks. The Bible plainly speaks about that."

This new settlement began with about eight or nine families, including Glen Yoder's family. A few of these families had arrived a year before the Schrock family, while others arrived a year and a half after the Schrocks. One such family who arrived after the Schrocks was Ura Yoder's family who came from Arkansas.

Once Joe and Rachel moved from Bowling Green, they began having meetings with other members of the settlement and a Baptist preacher. It was during one of these meetings that they were discovered by Petey Burkholder. The Schrocks, the Baptist preacher, Glen Yoder, Ura Yoder, and his son, Levi, were sitting at a table when Petey Burkholder and his wife stopped by for a visit. Being a bishop, Petey felt compelled to ask this group what they were doing. Burkholder said that communion was next Sunday, and the community would take action against them because of what their meeting signified. The community would be concerned with having everybody in good standing. Next Petey Burkholder asked Joe how he felt about the Bible discussion meetings and Joe told him that, like Glen Yoder, he had to be a follower of the Bible and not of man. This news upset Burkholder greatly, but Joe believed that Burkholder needed to finally know his true feelings. For almost a year, Joe and Rachel had been having these feelings that the Amish religion was not providing them with what they needed spiritually, rather they felt that the Amish religion was filling their lives with useless ordinances that were not leading them closer to God. In remembering that day with Petey Burkholder, Joe says, We didn't believe what the Yoders were doing was wrong, but we believed that the Amish and all the ordinances were aside from the Bible and the truth.î

The Schrocks had attended meetings in Bowling Green in order to help plan the new settlement. In attendance at one of the meetings was Rachel's brother-in-law, Jake Mast, who was not pleased with what he had heard, especially in regards to the plans the Yoders had formulated. Jake approached Rachel with a list that contained some of the ordinances of the new settlement, which were radical when compared to the ordinances of the Bowling Green settlement. Not knowing just how many changes they had agreed upon, Rachel counted over a dozen ordinances that had upset her brother-in-law. Jake Mast was upset that this new settlement was open to allowing the women to wear slippers year round, instead of having the summer footwear be slippers and the winter footwear be tall shoes. In addition, Mast was upset with the possibility that this group would consider using chain saws and rubber from old tires to wrap around the wheels of their wagons.

The ten years that Joe and Rachel lived in Bowling Green, Missouri, they had to follow rules set forth by a group of people who were constantly in conflict with each other. Many times the opposing sides were divided between those who came from Iowa, Ohio, and Indiana and those who were affiliated with the Swiss people.

As Rachel explains, "Both moved into Bowling Green. The Iowa, Ohio, and Indiana people were first".

"It was contrast," Joe further explains. "There was a fight there all the time. It was nothing but confusion and that was one of the reasons we began to search for the truth."

The constant confusion began to reveal to Joe and Rachel that those such as the Swiss were not as concerned with being spiritual, rather they were concerned with having their way in running the community. For the Schrocks, life was not about how to properly fulfill man made ordinances, instead they were trying to live the good family life and to follow God and his plan for them.

* * *

In August of 1983, an occurrence happened that signaled to Joe and Rachel that their time as Amish church members was coming to an end. Four months prior both Joe and Rachel began to feel a peace come over them that would give them the strength to continue on their search for truth. This peace aided them in August of 1983 when they and about 50 other Amish began work on the building of a new barn for the Schrocks' farm. This would be a busy day for everyone, what with the men building the barn and the women preparing a big meal for everyone. Next to the quaint house the Schrocks lived in, tables were set up. During the course of the day, different people approached Rachel asking her different questions. Even those in this barn-raising group who Joe and Rachel considered to be close friends questioned Rachel. Most of the questions revolved around Joe's and Rachel's observance of the ordinances. The entire day was incredibly stressful for the Schrocks because of the visible signs that indicated they were not strictly following the ordinances. What gave them away the most was the chain saw used in cutting the lumber. Certain members of the church stood around and talked about the modern convenience, setting Joe on edge. Recalling that day, Joe says, "It was like truth versus evil. It was among us all that day."

The interrogation of Rachel continued throughout the day. Different members of the church would say things such as, "We hear you're not strict anymore," or "You don't care about our Amish." Later in the day, the group of Amish brought forth The Ordinance Letter, which contained 400-600 do's and don't. Joe and Rachel were aware that such a list existed, but they had never seen it before because the Amish community in Bowling Green had never deemed it necessary. With Joe and Rachel's attempt at breaking away from Amish tradition, the strict Amish thought that the Schrocks needed to see the list. Joe saw the list as the Amish's attempt at fencing them in. But he saw the list as something else, too. For Joe, the list was a representation of the preoccupation with rules and this preoccupation, Joe believed, was keeping his family away from the true meaning of God. "We knew there were things in the Bible that the Amish could see if they weren't all so busy working, working, working, and trying to stay away from the world. They are missing the point of what the Gospel of Christ is really all about in the Bible," Joe states.

The barn raising occurred in August of 1983; the day when Petey Burkholder caught the Schrocks at the Yoder's with the Baptist preacher was in October of 1983; and two weeks later, the Schrocks made the conscious decision that they had to leave the Amish community. Though the Schrocks told their Amish community that they were not leaving, only that they were not going to be in church for awhile because of the difference in beliefs, they realized that the end of being Amish was near and that they were free to do as they pleased.

While the Schrocks felt that they were free, the Amish were not so willing to let them go out and worship in the fashion that they desired. After Joe and Rachel left the Amish, the community gathered together a group of preachers who would try to reason with the Schrocks. The first group of preachers went to Glen Yoder's, and Joe and Rachel were supposed to bring their own preachers who would defend them. To the Schrocks though, this seemed useless because they did not want to play reasoning games with the Amish. Glen Yoder advised Joe and Rachel not to give any answers that could not be supported with scripture text and to refrain from accusing the Amish of being inconsistent. The main thing for the Schrocks to do was to be as quiet as they could be, according to Glen Yoder.

Not only did the Amish try to convince Joe and Rachel to return to the church, but they also tried to prevent the Schrocks from worshipping God as they chose. The Schrocks and the Yoders decided to form their own circle of worshippers, but the Amish attempted to prevent them.

Using guilt as a way to sway those who try to leave is a main tactic of the Amish. They accomplish this by sending a group consisting of ministers and lay people to preach, cry, and wail to the lost soul. This tactic was used upon Joe and Rachel not long after they left their church. Joe remembers well what was said to them, "By the next Sunday they had Amish come up to keep us from starting our own church. I think that was the main motive of it and to admonish us." Her (Rachel's) dad started in with "Well, you know what we're here for and several of them started crying." With the tension growing thicker, Joe wanted to escape and leave these people to their sadness. Joe and Rachel were being pushed and prodded for answers on why they left and what their new found faith was based upon, but Rachel felt that there were no easy answers to the Amish's questions. How could a person answer in just one sentence a question that deals with one's faith and religion? Such a serious topic requires a lengthy answer because religion, to many people, and especially the Schrocks, is what they base their entire life upon. Rachel also felt that in answering the questions she would be condemning them to their face, which was not something she wanted to do. The questions and preaching continued for awhile, but when the group of Amish saw they were not going to convince the Schrocks to return, they left so that Joe and Rachel would have time to think over all the things that had been said to them.

Weekend after weekend, a group of Amish would come to try and convince Joe and Rachel to return to the Amish church. After the fourth weekend of visits, Joe and Rachel decided that they must take a stand. On this particular weekend, three relatives had been sent to stay with Joe and Rachel to try and prevent the Schrocks from participating in another church. But Joe and Rachel were tired of these various attempts of persuasion and coercion, so they decided to go with their children to the Yoder's house to have Sunday service. Joe informed his three brothers-in-law that they were welcome to go with them or suggested that they could go to their own church. The relatives climbed into a buggy and went on their way to their own church, and the Schrock family went to their church. What made these weekend visits more difficult was the fact that Joe and Rachel had such a small house, tiny in fact, and they had quite a large family. When they had these visitors, they had to sleep side by side. Joe would be so upset from these visits that he could not concentrate on his work. He says, "You couldn't think about your chores, your work. There's a lot of chores to do here. They are in the middle of it, milking to do, all these things to do and all they are here for is to try to convince us we are wrong."

One of the most difficult visits for Rachel was when her parents came to see them for the first time. Rachel did not want to say anything that would be painful to her parents, and this thought stayed on her mind. All she wanted to do was to hide in a closet to escape the tension caused by this visit. Through prayer, Rachel was able to overcome this difficult period of her life, and with each visit, she was able to feel more at peace with her decision to be a born again Christian.

* * *

Eventually the visits from the Amish ended, and Joe and Rachel were left alone to practice the type of Christianity they thought was right for them. Since they made the decision to leave, Joe and Rachel have tried to keep in contact with those members of their family who have remained Amish. The first few months after they left were difficult, for their families did not even want to see them, but most of the family members have grown to accept Joe and

93

Rachel's new life. Even though there are family members who have come to accept Joe and Rachel for who they are, the Amish's treatment of the Schrocks is cold and sometimes harsh. A few will venture so far as to speak with Joe and Rachel, but the family members do not want to be asked any questions. Those family members who have not been able to accept Joe and Rachelís new life shun the Schrocks. Among the Amish, the tendency to shun is described as "shunning with a vengeance," which is meant to hurt those who are being shunned. Joe's brothers shun them, while Rachel, likewise, has two brothers who shun with a vengeance.

Rachel's family tends to be more severe in showing disapproval for her and Joe's departure from the Amish church. At a funeral, Rachel was treated coldly compared to her sister who left the Amish for the Mennonite religion. Though the Amish do not approve of their members leaving the church for any other religion, it is more acceptable to be Mennonite than to be English. This is so because the English are too worldly and will defend their country and loved ones in case of war, while the Mennonites are less worldly and continue to have such practices as the wearing of the covering by the women.

* * *

Though Joe and Rachel have suffered through much heartache, they are now happy and successful. Joe works in construction doing remodeling jobs, and he farms. Rachel home schools those children who are still living at home. Among their children, the Schrocks have sons who are ministers, a son who is a missionary in Russia, and a daughter who is studying to be an elementary school teacher. To complete their life, Joe and Rachel have a spiritual fulfillment that comes from knowing Christ and knowing God's will. Today Joe and Rachel are still members of the Philadelphia Baptist Church in Philadelphia, Missouri; the church they joined after they left the Amish. Rachel especially has enjoyed her new religion because she has a new freedom. Equality and freedom of expression are two of the things Rachel can enjoy now that she has left the Amish religion.

Now that Joe and Rachel are no longer Amish, they are now considered by their former Amish community as ex-Amish. As ex-Amish members, Joe and Rachel live a life that is no different from that of an average American. They use electricity, wear the clothes of the English, and drive cars. Though the Schrocks have a new-found freedom, they keep this freedom in perspective. They do not drink or smoke or curse, instead they live their lives like the solid Christians that they are. While the Amish have tried to scare Joe and Rachel into believing that their souls will be forsaken when they die because they are no longer Amish, both know the real truth. No longer do the Schrocks have to suffer under the oppression that is the Amish religion. Through their struggles, Joe and Rachel have discovered that with knowledge comes power.

Chapter Nine
Levi and Miriam

Miriam Mullet awoke before dawn with a feeling of antici-pation that something special was about to happen. In all her twen-ty-one years she had never felt this way before. She pressed her face against the cool glass and looked out over the small Amish settlement of Kenton, Ohio. It was a Saturday so she wouldn't have to teach school, but she had numerous other chores to accomplish before today was done. The day was going to be hot, and the work would be hard, but she wanted it to begin anyway.

She made her bed quickly and went downstairs to prepare breakfast for her family. Mother was already seated at the table kneading bread dough. Miriam said her good morning and began her routine.

Around nine-thirty she walked down the drive to the mailbox. It held a circular from the Dollar Store and a small white envelope addressed in an unfamiliar hand. A shock swept through her from head to toe. Levi Yoder from Bowling Green, Missouri was writing to her!

Levi and his brother had been in Kenton last summer visiting friends at the settlement on their way back from their grandfather's home in Ashland. Levi had noticed Miriam at church services. Miriam noticed Levi right back. It was 1969.

Miriam raced to the house and into her room. She examined the envelope for a long time before opening it. It contained one small, lined sheet of paper. It wasn't so much what the letter said as the tenderness behind his words that convinced Miriam on the spot that he was the one.

Miriam replied, and the two exchanged letters often over the next several weeks. When she wrote that she had an opportunity to come to Bowling Green to work for a young mother with five children, Levi was elated. They could see each other every Sunday!

When Miriam had to return to Kenton in order to teach school, Levi vowed to visit in the fall. Their courtship was completely honorable and their desire to remain respectable was apparent to the community. They wrote each other frequently over the winter and spring months, and Miriam was again offered the opportunity to resume her position as mother's assistant the following summer. Once again, Levi visited in the fall. The following summer Levi asked Miriam to be his wife.

Levi's father was a bishop in the Amish church, and he performed the wedding ceremony at Miriam's family home on September 20, 1973. All of her pupils came, as well as the entire community. Miriam's mother feared that the food would run out!

They both worked harvesting apples along with Miriam's sister Irene until November. They were paid a flat rate for each bushel they picked, so Miriam and Irene raced against each other to see who could earn the most money. One day Miriam picked 104 bushels to beat Irene's record!

The happy couple left shortly afterwards for Missouri. Levi worked on his father's farm for three years, and Miriam gave birth to two sons. Because it was understood that the family farm would be inherited by his youngest sister, when the opportunity to form a carpenter partnership with his brother-in-law- arose, Levi accepted even though it would mean moving his family to Fredericktown, Ohio. Miriam was expecting their third child. It was March, 1977.

According to Amish traditions, the youngest daughter (or in a few cases the youngest son) inherits the family homestead. While seeming unfair to English culture, this arrangement has very practical implications to the parents. Because Amish women continue to have children until menopause, parents could well be in their sixties or beyond when the youngest child reaches maturity. Such a tradition provides a guarantee of care during the parents' last years. Many times a separate house is constructed adjacent to or even as an extension of the original structure. This is commonly referred to as a "grandfather house." By the time the property is deeded to the desnated benefactor, the parents are often grandparents.

After the move, Levi began to have questions about the Amish faith in spite of the fact that his carpentry business was flourishing and his family life was happy and stable. Although he discussed his concerns with a co-worker, he and Miriam rarely discussed his feelings. Levi would, however, frequently question the content of the sermons at their church in conversations with Miriam.

In 1978, Levi and Miriam bought a forty acre farm after a prosperous period in the carpentry business. They lived with Miriam's sister and brother-in-law until they could build a house, a barn and some other outbuildings in 1979. Miriam and Levi describe this as a particularly happy period in their lives.

Shortly afterwards, the seventy acre farm adjacent to them became available, so they purchased it as well. With one hundred and ten acres to farm and a carpentry career, Levi began to lease the farm to his brother-in-law. The new addition to their land already had an existing house and barn.

After the birth of their fourth child, their only daughter, Miriam became friends with a neighbor woman. Mary H. was was of the Methodist faith. This neighbor proved to be very influential on Miriam's own beliefs. They shared thoughts and ideas at first, then her new friend began to share religious literature with Miriam. She was particularly impressed with The Calvary Road by Roy Heston and The Tabernacle by Dr. Martin DeHand. The works of John R. Rice and Norman Vincent Peale also especially appealed to Miriam. She consumed the literature and could not find anything with which to disagree. Levi was aware that Miriam was reading materials which the Amish church would deem dangerous, but was not concerned enough to discuss it with her as he was continuing to doubt the ways of the Amish as well.

Levi continued to question items in the sermons and realized that when he had been exposed to other Amish settlements, even as a youngster, he was taken aback by each community's belief that theirs was the only perfect settlement. He found the condescension between the communities unsettling and somewhat ridiculous. He questioned also the Amish idea of seclusion and the prohibition from sharing their faith with others in a missionary manner. Why shouldn't their faith be shared if it was indeed the correct path?

Neither Levi nor Miriam had considered ever leaving the Amish faith or the Amish way of life at this point, but Levi did begin to discuss his feelings more with his wife. Miriam found her true faith in 1979. She was born again into the body of Christ and maintains her faith to this day. That summer she felt that life was different than it used to be. She felt calmer and began to question many things that the Amish considered sinful. She could not reconcile her own thoughts with those of the Amish. She did not discuss her feelings with Levi right away, but tried to persuade him to read the materials that she was reading.

Levi attempted to assuage his conscience with statistics. He felt that because crime was non-existent and divorce unheard of in the Amish community that they must be doing something right. The logic of the sermons, however, continued to bother him. There was so much emphasis on the order of the church, and he found the order of the church to be insufficient. One minister even stated If any man be here even now that would be keeping all the commandments of the church, the order of the church, and yet wouldn't believe in it, then it wouldn't do him any good. Levi realized that he was just such a man.

Levi began to talk to Miriam about his convictions. Miriam was afraid to leave the stability of the church and her family. In spite of her own religious experiences, she was still thankful to be a part of the Amish community - particularly after exposure to the outside world. She told Levi that they should concentrate on their home, their family.

Levi talked frequently with another neighbor whose brother was a Baptist minister. They made plans for Levi to meet the brother for some friendly discussions of the scriptures. The minister also happened to be a licensed pilot. Levi remembered the time he was tricked into taking a short airplane ride.

Although the Amish do not allow ownership of motor vehicles or driving, they will frequently hire a car and driver so that they can ride as passengers. This is particularly true when a trip becomes necessary that is impractical to attempt on horseback or in a buggy. Because of the nature of his business, Levi came in contact with many outsiders to the Amish community. One of Levi's English friends had a plane and wanted Levi to go up in it with him. Levi responded that the Amish do not fly.

This friend coaxed him into taxiing around the runway. Levi did not see the harm in riding in the airplane as long as it remained on the ground. His friend, however, decided to take matters in his own hands and give Levi a thrill. Perhaps he thought that once Levi experienced flying he would be more open to other forbidden experiences. Maybe he just had a mean streak and wanted to see Leviís reaction. Maybe he simply did not understand the significance of the Amish restriction against flying.

Although he was very frightened at first, Levi realized that his only option was to trust the pilot to get him safely on the ground. After all, he couldn't very well jump out of the plane. The sensation was incredible: fear, exhilaration, wonder, and awe combined with an unbelievable feeling of reverence. He couldn't get over how small everything appeared. He wondered if this was how humans appeared to God.

When Levi met the minister and they began to discuss the scriptures, Levi found him to be a very learned Bible scholar. Miriam engaged this minister in religious discussion as well. She described him as being very knowledgeable about erroneous interpretations of the scriptures. After studying Romans 8 one day in October of 1983, Levi too was saved. "For whosoever shall call upon the name of the Lord shall be saved." This seemed so simple and pure.

The Yoders' decided to take a trip to visit Levi's family in Missouri. The Baptist minister asked if he could tag along. During their stay, the minister conducted an informal Bible study meeting at Levi's father's home. Ura Yoder was having his own doubts about the Amish faith in spite of his status as bishop. Levi's brother, Glen, was also in attendance. Another bishop from the local community happened to stop by unexpectedly. When he discovered that the group was in the middle of a Bible study meeting, he was shocked and upset. He condemned them all and threatened to write to Levi and Miriam's bishop back in Ohio.

The Amish generally confront their wayward members by intimidation. The bishop, and ministers, deacon will approach the member when he is alone and very much outnumbered. Because the reverse of this situation was occurring here, the bishop was on unfamiliar territory. When the Baptist minister began to question him about the Bible and involved him in discussion of interpretations of the scriptures, the bishop was ill prepared to meet the challenge. The Baptist minister mopped up the floor with the unready bishop.

Levi and Miriam decided to sell their farm and mentioned this fact to some friends. One of them knew of a family from Pennsylvania who was in town looking for a farm to buy. Levi and Miriam feared that they must sell the farm as quickly as possible because they had been discovered. Their only hope was to sell the farm before the letter from Missouri arrived. Miraculously, the transaction was made before the sun went down that same day. They remained in the settlement for two months following the sale and their announcement of their intentions to leave the Amish.

Levi had been communicating with his father, the bishop and sensed that his father was having conflicts about the Amish doctrine also. One month after they left the church, Levi's father left as well.

Elders of the church came in groups to try and dissuade the Yoders from leaving. Because they had to remain in the community for the time being, they continued to dress in the Amish fashion and conduct their business as usual. Miriam's parents also came to try to persuade them to change their minds. Their friends accused them of leaving just because they wanted a car.

The Baptist Minister who has been involved in Miriam and Levi's leaving the Amish, pastored a church in Berea, KY. After much thought, Levi & Miriam decided to move to Berea, KY and attend the Baptist church of the minister. After they arrived in Berea, Levi purchased an old gas station & food store as an investment and had intentions of continuing in his profession as a carpenter. However, the store demanded so much more attention and money that Levi and Miriam had to work full-time in the store.

When Miriam's father died, they returned to attend the funeral. In spite of being under the ban, Miriam and Levi and their children were received moderately well. They were denied their rightful place in the family lineup, but were still allowed to sit with the family.

Both Levi and Miriam indicate that they might not have left the Amish if only the two of them were to be considered. They had found their faith and were secure in it even within the Amish community. This would have required a great deal of restraint on their part, but it could have been accomplished. They stress that because they had to go outside the Amish religion to be saved, to find their faith, they knew that their children would likely have to do the same. A difficult task indeed. They felt compelled to leave primarily for the sake of their children's salvation.

At Miriam's father's funeral, the eldest sons stood their ground when confronted by a bishop. One of their sons is in the seminary. One son is studying for another church-related vocation. Their daughter is preparing to be a youth minister, and the two youngest sons are still in school. The Yoder family are all members of the First Baptist Church in Richmond, Ky.

Levi admits, in his understated way, that he feels much freer to demonstrate his affection for his wife. Previously, he felt very constrained against showing his feelings. Both emphasize how wonderful it is to be working together in the store and spending more time with one another. They are obviously very proud of all their children.

Chapter Ten
The Yoders

It was 1983 when Ura Yoder, along with his wife, two of their sons, one of their daughters, and their spouses, left the Amish. Now almost 80 years old, Ura, a small man with white hair who still wears his Amish beard looks back on that time with sadness, but not regret. In his own words, Ura explains, "I never regretted in my heart, but I still had to struggle with it in my nature."

Ura I. Yoder grew up in the Amish, but he did not join the church until he was 23 years old. His sons, Glen, Levi and Ivan often joke that one reason their father joined the church was to marry Edna Christner. Ura was, by Amish standards, a bit of a rebellious teenager; he even played the guitar, something that is not looked upon favorably by the Amish. He had to give up the guitar when he joined the church and did not pick it up again until he left the Amish.

In 1941, at the age of 24, Ura and Edna were married in the Amish church. The Yoders had five children: three sons and two daughters. By 1983, all of the Yoder's children except one daughter had also left the Amish. Ura was a church member until 1968, when he went beyond mere member status and became a minister through the Amish lot system. The lot system is used when choosing a minister, and it includes every married male member of the church. The members of the church vote for the man that they want as minister, by walking by a room of current ministers and whispering the name of their choice. Once all of the members have voted, the votes are tallied, and every man with at least three votes goes to the next phase of the lot system. During this phase, there are books placed on a table and each man picks a book. There is only one book with a mark or a piece of paper in it, and the one man who picks that book is the minister. Although the Amish do not believe in men receiving a calling to preach, they do believe that God leads the right man to be the minister by means of the lot.

When choosing a bishop, the lot system is done a little differently. The three ministers are the only members eligible for the position of bishop. Again, there are books laid out on a table, and the men each choose one. Usually they start with the oldest minister. There is only one book with a mark in it, and the man who picks that book becomes the bishop. Three years after becoming a minister, through another lot drawing, Ura became a bishop. Even though he would not admit it to any other Amish person at the time, Ura felt called to this position.

"Even when I was ordained to be a bishop, again there were things that happened. Well, things I can't relate to even; too many things I've forgotten, but there were quite a few things that were miracles. One thing, they have books, each one has a book and they are in a lot. Each one has a book and there are three in a lot, and I'm the oldest, so I go up first to pick up my book. I reached up there, and out of the blue I did not get the book I wanted. As I reached for the book, my fingernail...caught the edge of the corner of the book and knocked it over and it fell on the floor and rolled plum over to the bishop who was in the lead that day, rolled right in front of him and that's where it landed. A book roll! I couldn't imagine it. That book rolled over to him. I just, oh, I knew. Paul Byler was so burdened that day; he felt like it was going to be him that day and I did too.So when I reached for that book and couldn't get it, I thought oh, it's Paul's. That's his book. So I took the next one. As I went back to my place, I came past the bishop that had picked the first book up, and he handed it to me. I had two books; I didn't want two books."

So, Ura took the two books, careful not to get them mixed up, and replaced the book that had fallen for Paul to choose, which he did, but, as it turned out, Ura's book had the lot and Paul's did not.

"Paul went up and got it. That was my book, I fully believe it."

Ura accepted the position as bishop with both the thankfulness and the humility necessary by Amish standards, "In my heart I was thankful, but at the same time, I felt so undeserving to be in the lead of the church." Ura then began to study the Bible more in order

106

to better serve the church, studying the English translations as well as the German translation used exclusively by the Amish church.

Four years before Ura became a bishop in 1970, his older son Ivan left the Amish, leaving behind his wife, one son and two daughters. He left without telling anyone in his family because he saw no real future in the Amish. "The family was more a part of the church than they were of me," he said. Naturally, Ivan was placed in the ban, meaning that other Amish people could not eat at the same table with him, and were hardly allowed to speak to him. Even though Ura did not know exactly when Ivan was excommunicated because Ivan was in another church district, Ura and the rest of the family shunned Ivan whenever he was around them. Because this was so uncomfortable, Ivan eventually stopped coming around his family, but he did keep in touch with them. Ivan and his family lived in Orange County in southern Indiana, and though he admits that he was in contact with his parents more, he continued having some contact with his ex-wife.

After Ivan left, the church helped care for his wife and children. Ivan and his wife were divorced in 1974, and he does pay child support, although receiving and keeping that money has left his ex-wife in bad standing with the church. She is in the ban, but she remains among the Amish. Ivan's children are not Amish; his daughters actually drive automobiles. Ivan writes to his children regularly, but he does not see them. "My ex-wife doesn't want them to have anything to do with me," he says. Ivan was completely unaware of his father's move to leave the Amish. In 1983, he received an invitation to his sister Mattie's wedding. Mattie, Ura's youngest child was marrying a young man by the name of John Bontrager who was also from Bowling Green, Missouri. Ivan did not go for fear of spoiling the event for his sister because he was in the ban. He was actually confused about even getting this invitation. The wedding was one of the last events to take place before the Yoders left the Amish. Mattie sent Ivan the invitation knowing what was coming, but Ivan did not know and did not attend the wedding.

Ivan was unaware that his father had been preaching of things the Amish did not agree with, and he did not know that his brother, Glen, had met with a Baptist pastor and was also questioning the Amish faith. He had no idea that his family, along with several other families, had been spending a great deal of time studying and discussing the Bible. Ivan had no idea that his entire immediate family—with the exception of one sister—was planning to leave the Amish church.

The decision to leave was not a sudden one for some of the Yoders. Glen and Levi knew that they would have to leave; Ura did not want to leave, but the Amish church left him and his wife no choice. Ura does not feel that he actually made any decision, except to preach the truth as he understands it from studying the Bible. The church excommunicated him.

"Before I was in the ministry, it (reading the Bible) wasn't quite so extensive," Ura admits, "but, after I got into the ministry, I got into studying the Bible really deep; and that, according to the Amish, was my fault."

"When one reads and studies the Bible too deeply, that gets you off the Amish," Ura says. The Amish do not like for their members to read the Bible too closely.

"The church frowns on it if you say too much," Ura explains, "they believe in the Bible, believe in Christ, and I love them, but they didn't like it if you studied too much."

The more he read and studied, the more he learned and understood, and the more he questioned the Amish faith. "I was just studying the scriptures' true meaning, and found things that did not harmonize with our Amish doctrine or teaching," Ura explains.

Then Ura began preaching about some of the things he found in the Bible. Ura read the English Bible, and in Colossians Chapter 2, Verse 20, it says, "Wherefore if ye be dead with Christ from the rudiments of the world, why, as though living in the world, are ye subject to ordinances." This scripture forced him to question the meaning of the Amish ordinances.

"I knew that our church was composed of ordinances very much," Ura says. "We spend whole days in drafting ordinances."

When he learned that such ordinances are not necessary, he began preaching that, even though it went against the Amish beliefs.

Ura also preached that the Pharisees were not just self-righteous, but also very religious. He went so far as to compare the Pharisees to the Amish. Levi, to explain this connection, quotes the Apostle Paul from Romans saying, "I bear witness, they have a zeal for God, but not the knowledge." And, even though the younger Amish church members liked Ura and his style of preaching, the older Amish did not, as he challenged some of their beliefs.

The other scripture that caused Ura to greatly question the Amish faith is found in the fifteenth chapter of Matthew which says "But in vain they do worship me, teaching for doctrines the commandments of men." That scripture moved Ura as he saw that the Amish "took the commandments of the men and made out of them a doctrine for the church to live by". He saw that the Amish church was doing just that and that was not what God intended. And, according to the Amish, if one does not follow their rules (not God's rules) to the letter, Levi explains, "It would ultimately set you at total odds with the church where you would be dis-fellowshipped, or excommunicated." But the Yoders chose to follow their hearts and the teachings of God as the teachings became clear to them through reading an English translation of the Bible.

Ura's wife Edna warned him of the trouble that his preaching would cause, and Ura himself feared what the church would do to him if he kept preaching in the way that he was, but teaching the truth was important to him.

"I wanted to preach the Word!" Ura states. "Sincerely wanted to preach the Word, because that's what I was ordained to do. And the Bible told me if I preach to please the people, I'm not a servant of Christ."

His preaching put questions in the minds of some of the other church members, not just his family, and this led to Bible studies and discussions when these people got together outside of the church, though this was done quietly for about a year.

"He could explain scriptures in a way to really hold the church members attention," Levi explains. "He had a gift of communication that most of the Amish don't have."

Still the movement to leave the Amish was spearheaded by his son, Glen. Glen Yoder was born in 1950, and at the age of two and a half he was stricken with polio, which left him crippled. Because of polio, Glen could not farm as most Amish men do. Instead, to make a living, Glen taught in the Amish school. Glen married Ida Bontreger in 1973, and he helped to raise the family that they had together. Because Glen could not do many physical things, he exercised his mind more than other Amish men, more than the Amish would have wanted. He studied the Bible and began to question what he found, as what he found conflicted with what he had been taught as a boy. And even though Glen could not tell any of the Amish, he felt a genuine calling to preach the Word of God.

The Amish purposely keep their people at an eighth grade education level. They feel that too much education is a bad thing, probably because it causes people to question too much. The Amish also preach from the German translation of the Bible. The Amish do not even speak German, but a splicing of German and Pennsylvania Dutch. Church goers cannot fully understand the German Bible as it is read to them. Because many of the Amish people cannot understand German, the leaders of the church are looked to for translation, and the Bible says what they want it to, making the Amish way of life seem like the only way to get to Heaven. Everyone keeps repeating what they have been told for years and years, and many don't bother to look for themselves. But the Yoders did.

The more Glen studied the English Bible, the more he had questions, as did his father. Ura recalls as a child of seven or eight asking his brother if the Amish were in the Bible, and when his brother told him that the Amish were not in the Bible, Ura remembers feeling terribly disappointed and let down. Ura admits that he was already then considering the grounds of what they were doing. Comparing the scriptures with the English Bible, made more sense to Ura and Glen, and caused them to question the Amish faith more and more. Glen even befriended a Baptist pastor in his quest for answers. This pastor explained many things to Glen, and as the Bible became clearer to him, Glen challenged others to read and study more, especially his brother Levi.

Glen was so sure of his stance, he would often have the Baptist pastor over to his home to discuss the Bible with his family and friends. Ida admits that the times when the pastor was over were the only times that she was afraid of the Amish reaction. Reading the Bible is not against the Amish faith, although they believe one should not read it too much. But, listening to and believing a minister of another faith was certainly against the Amish faith, and was grounds for being placed in the ban. However, by the time that their meetings came out into the open, Ida says that she was relieved to be done with the hiding.

The Bible studies took place in either Glen's or Ura's home, and included several of the family's friends also, about six other families. These people did not originally meet to study the Bible, they were just visiting one another and began discussing questions they had about the Amish church and faith. Ura's son Levi came from Ohio to the Maywood area of Missouri to visit with family and friends and to discuss the Bible.

The Yoders and their friends were visiting and discussing the Bible in Ura's home the evening that everything came out into the open. That evening by accident another one of the area's bishops came into the house and walked in on a meeting with a Baptist pastor. A bit of a biblical debate ensued between the Baptist pastor and the Amish bishop. According to Levi, the Baptist pastor was totally prepared to defend his position. He had a defense to make in front of everyone and he was prepared. The bishop voiced his disapproval of this meeting and how this was wrong according to his beliefs and his interpretation of the Bible. The Baptist pastor pretty much plowed him under, proving him wrong with quotes from the Bible. When the bishop threatened the Yoders with the ban, they responded with no fear, and this left the bishop not knowing what to do. He became uncomfortable and did not stay long, but unfortunately that confrontation started everything instead of finishing it.

Glen and Ida were not afraid that night, even though they were aware of what would happen. Ida was actually glad that the hiding was over. Ura felt that he was not completely aware of what happened that night; he did not comprehend the magnitude of the evening. Ura did not want to leave the Amish; he had no problem with the Amish lifestyle, and he had several life-long friends, but once he was excommunicated, his feelings about the Amish doctrine would not allow him to return to the church.

After the bishop left Ura's house that night, action against the Yoders' was not taken immediately. The next time the bishop confronted the Yoders he brought a couple of ministers with him. In most cases, when confronting a wayward church member, the church leaders come as a group. Feeling outnumbered by this intimidation, the member will usually submit to their will. For the Yoder family, this did not work. They felt the Lord was leading them and that their decision was based on the Bible, the will of God.

The other area bishops did not decide upon a shunning until a month later. Levi had returned to Ohio, and he and his wife, Miriam, sold their farm before they were placed in the ban by the bishop in their area. The bishop from Missouri had sent a letter to the bishop in Levi's settlement explaining what had happened.

It is important to know that the Yoder family left for religious reasons, because of religious disagreements with the Amish doctrine. Levi voiced confusion to an Amish bishop later about how the Bible says that Christians should go out and win people to Christ, and that the Amish do not practice this. The Amish bishop replied that people who had no ties to the Amish were not the concern of the Amish, and it was not their responsibility to save the non-Amish.

Ura explains the overall family stance best. "If I had went for power, equipment, everything- all those privileges; if I had went for that, a thousand times I would have already went back; but I don't think it's worth it..If the Amish way was the way to get there, to get that free trip to Heaven, why I certainly would not swap it for a tractor."

Ura's children—especially Glen—feel that if people were not meant to have electricity, or running water, or cars, then that would be taught in the Bible, and it is not. But, overall, the Yoders leaving was not discontent with the Amish way of life; it was about not agreeing with the religious doctrine of the Amish.

The Yoders were eventually placed in the ban, and the Amish bishops wanted to handle this situation in the Amish way—the Yoders finding three ministers to defend them to three other ministers to defend the views of the church. The Yoders knew that they would not find three ministers to agree with them, so they did not try. The Amish then chose six ministers and confronted the Yoders. They were bombarded with many dire warnings before that ordeal was all over. The Amish could never decide what to do with the Yoders (Ura and Glen and their families) because they never spoke out against the Amish church during this questioning. The Amish finally decided to give the Yoders three weeks to redeem themselves and get "back in order" or they would be excommunicating themselves—removing any guilt from the Amish church.

The final straw for the Amish church was when a member of the church, who had been placed in the ban and had left the church, bought some hay from the Yoders. When questioned, Ura told the church that he did not know what had gone on, but his sons had made a deal with this ex-church member concerning the sale. "I purposely didn't know. I tried not to know," Ura explains.

Basically, as Ura says, "I didn't shun him like the Amish church thought I should." Ura also points out that the church had been paying particularly close attention to him, looking for a fault, waiting for him to slip. "They really watched what I did, every move I made," Ura said. "I'd venture to say, it I watch you like that, I'd see mistakes every once in a while."

Three weeks went by and the Yoders were not swayed; they were excommunicated. "They illuminated the mistakes, made it look big, and cried out in church that it was so bad, what I did," Ura says. "I still don't have a conscience that it was that wrong."

As an interesting twist, when the Yoders left the church, they did not leave the area; the rest of the Amish did. In fact, the Yoders still live in the house that they did when they were excommunicated. The Amish forced them out of the church, and then the Amish left the area.

Reuniting with Ivan was a joyous occasion. For the first time since he had left the Amish in 1970, Ivan sat at a dinner table with his family, and they were allowed to talk to him. All without fear of reprimand by the Amish church.

"I sat and ate with my family for the first time in thirteen years," Ivan said. "I could hardly swallow the food. It was very touching and special to be back."

Another interesting detail to the Yoders' story is that Ivan began attending church again around the time that the Yoders started studying the Bible intensely, and he received the Lord into his heart around the time that the rest of his family was going through their experience. Unfortunately, this family reunion was incomplete.

One of the Yoders' daughters had stayed with the Amish, and she was killed in an accident after the Yoders left. The Amish did not inform the family; the Yoders found out from some neighbors they knew from that Indiana area. Glen had heard Paul Harvey on the radio tell about an accident involving an Amish buggy being run over by an 18-wheeler; he knew that it occurred in southern Indiana, the area where his sister lived. Talking to those neighbors only confirmed the Yoders' fears. It was their daughter and sister, who had been killed in that accident, leaving her husband to raise their eleven children. The Yoders did attend the funeral, but of course they were shunned by all of the Amish, including their son-in-law, and they were unable to comfort their grandchildren.

Despite the sadness that the family experienced in leaving behind life-long friends and losing a sister and daughter, the Yoders are all successful and happy in their lives.

"I'm sorry, terribly sorry that it made a lot of grief," Ura says. "To think, for all of the friends we sacrificed."

After being excommunicated from the Amish church, they received a mail-out from the Philadelphia Baptist Church, an invitation to a special ordination service where a new pastor was to be ordained.

Having had serious doubts concerning the Amish method of ordaining their ministers by lot where many a man was elected who had no calling to preach or gift to minister, I knew I wanted to witness this ordination. Three of us couples hired a driver to take us to church. This was the first time any of us attended a non-Amish worship service. Hesitantly, in our full Amish garb, we entered the auditorium.

Coming from Texas, never having seen Amish before, Reverend Tim Stow felt sure we were "hecklers" undoubtedly here to cause a disturbance to interfere with his ordination. Later he admitted how he refused to come shake hands with us but instead sent one of the visiting Pastors.

We stayed for the carry-in meal and found opportunity to ask the guest preacher doctrinal questions on the sermon we heard. Sensing our sincere thirst for truth and need for Bible instruction, he advised Pastor Stowe to follow up on us at once. Bright and early the next morning together they came out to our home for a visit. Immediately a weekly Bible study was planned for Tuesday evenings.

The sweet memories of our spiritual growth in these meetings are constant reminders even now of the wonderful grace of our God.

We were deeply impressed with the proceedings of that ordination service, how the candidate was asked over 80 doctrinal questions and answered each one with a Bible answer using many scriptural references, quoting chapter and verse by heart. I thank God that the thirty plus people of us (6 families) are still, 15 years later, all attending Bible believing churches.

When they first left the Amish, Ura did some preaching for the Philadelphia Baptist Church in Philadelphia, Missouri, but he now lives more like a retiree, playing his guitar for his own enjoyment and for others. He even makes some spare change now and then from passersby.

Ura's children have also experienced success. Today Mattie and John and their three children share a large 2-story home with Mattie's parents. Mattie's family lives on the second floor. Mattie and John find this arrangement to their liking as Mattie says, "My parents are in their 80's and sometimes need a little assistance, not much though. Both are still actively involved in their daily activities, and its nice to be able to talk to them whenever I like." Mattie also home schools her three children, two boys and a little girl, who happens to be as sweet as sugar. We teach our children Christian values; this is very fulfilling and wondrous time in our lives.

Their father John, works as an Auctioneer in Bowling Green, Missouri, the area from which he came. Now he returns to do his daily job. The local bishops got together and insisted that John be fired, because no self respecting Amish would dare accept an Auctioneer who was X-Amish. The owner of the auction house, to the dismay of the local Amish leaders, refused, saying no, to their demands.

The Amish ordered their men not to attend any auction where John was working. This caused a lot of hard feelings among the Amish themselves, because the Amish men love to attend the weekly auction, mostly in order to catch up on the local gossip and lounge around the auction house. Even to this day an occasional Amish man will show up for the auction, of course hoping no other Amish sees him.

Ivan has since been remarried and now drives a semi-truck for a living.

Levi, who resides in Kentucky, owns and operates a food mart with a mechanic's garage attached.

Glen Yoder is perhaps the happiest of all. His calling to become a minister became a reality for him two years after he left the

Amish. He has now been preaching at the Community Baptist Church in Palmyra, Missouri ten years. Glen also runs a tour service taking tourists on horse and buggy rides around Hannibal, Missouri, showing off the historical sites portrayed in Tom Sawyer and Huckleberry Finn. In addition to all of that, Glen and Ida take in foster children, sharing their home and their love with those who need it most.

Glen and Ida do travel to Northern Iowa periodically so that Ida can keep in contact with her family. In order to visit her family, they must dress in Amish clothes. They do this so that Ida can stay in touch with her mother, so that she does not lose her family totally. But, all in all, Glen and Ida are happy. In fact, right choices always bring happiness. They made the right choice based on what the Bible says, and they do not regret that choice. It is the fifth chapter of Isaiah that says, "Woe unto them that call the right wrong and the wrong right." The Yoders live without woe.

"I have a hard time," Ura admits. "But, no way would I consider going back. I just couldn't believe in it."

Open Letter From Eli

This is a letter from a brother to his family members who left the Amish. Eli was grateful for the opportunity to express his feelings.He only asked that we correct his spelling and punctuation; as he said, "I am not a book writer." We agreed to his wishes. Here is his letter:

We are of the Amish faith, and we've got family that has left the Amish for over 26 years already and it still hurts! Just to think of all the heartaches it's caused our dear Mom and Dad. I still claim them as my brothers etc. as far as visiting with them etc. But from the bottom of my heart I wish that they'd never left, as the family is broken up. Still they could repent and come back and we all would rejoice. As the way it is we have to shun them, which hurts.

When they first left it really was hard to accept for the family and friends. As time went on, it more or less sort of wore off; I think more so for the church, but for the family not so much. Still it just sort of wore off etc.

I have really NO reason to believe that anyone has a reason to leave.They mostly want to blame this guy or preachers or whoever, parents or Dad. But when it all comes down to brass tacks, that still did not give them a good excuse, as all they'd had to do was what was right regardless.

I know my dad didn't hit the best, but that really doesn't give them the right to not do what's right.

I'm so thankful that we aren't to judge, as Who are we to judge? How do we know that we are saved? Just because we stayed Amish does not make us perfect.
This is a free world-each has to live for themselves; after that they come up to the age that they are old enough to know what's right from wrong.

I don't really think that any Amish can leave, that they don't wish themselves back, sooner or later. I wish it was just a dream that they ever left. But they are either too stubborn or just can't get enough will power to face the facts.

I guess all in all, I wish from the bottom of my heart that it would have never happened that anyone ever left the Amish, but try harder to do what we're taught.

Sincerely,

Eli

Conclusion

Amish try very hard to hide the flaws that reside in their community. But just like the rest of society, Amish must deal with crimes that are committed against each other and against the English. There are Amish in prisons in Wisconsin for rape, in Minnesota for tax fraud, in Pennsylvania for murder and drug dealing, Illinois for child molesting, Indiana for drugs, and Texas, Ohio, and other states for various crimes.

In most cases these criminals are caught because someone other than Amish turned them over to the proper authorities. Neu Leben has discovered in certain types of crimes, especially crimes against children, there are cover ups by the Amish leaders, bishops, ministers and deacons. The worst part of this is the parents of these children are sometimes covering up crimes that the other parent may be committing against one of their own children. Amish are not immune to the evils of the world.

What can be done to help these children? As in most cases, education would be a definite benefit, but the Amish are allowed to rule their own school system. Amish children only have to go to school through the eighth grade. In these Amish schools, the teachers are usually young Amish girls, unmarried, from 17 years of age and up. They have no formal training for teaching school, handling cases of abuse or even recognizing it. The Amish do not teach sex education in schools.

After a year of traveling across the country to many different Amish communities, interviewing former Amish and Amish, we have gathered many hours of video and audio tapes.

In some cases, the violence of certain crimes was unbelievable: spousal abuse, child abuse, various types of sexual abuses to both sexes, beatings that went beyond discipline and corrections.

119

Where do these children turn? They are taught when they are small not to trust outside people, English, as they are called. To the Amish children, the boogie man is an English person. I have heard parents tell their children if they don't do what they are told to do, an English person will come take them away. I've personally driven to Amish homes and seen Amish children hide. Now, of course, once they know who you are, that is a different story. Like all children, they too are curious; they love to look at your car or van and best of all look at the strange English person.

I believe children should have certain responsibilities as they grow up; it helps to build character, but the Amish take this notion to an extreme. Young children are asked to do very dangerous types of farm labor, and most time left unsupervised. When children are told at a young age to get up with the sun and work till dark like an adult, there will be accidents, even death. The death of a young child is senseless, no children should be put in a position that could cost them their life. All you have to do is read the Amish weekly papers; every week somewhere a young child is killed doing adult work. I've read the Budget which comes out of Sugarcreek, Ohio and Die Botschaft which comes out of Lancaster, Pennsylvania and every week one or more accidents occur where either a child is killed or crippled or they lose their arm or leg. This is truly sad.

The Amish always enjoy pointing their fingers at the English ways. They say their schools rate higher than the English schools; Amish parents have no problems with their children smoking pot or drinking beer and that theirs is a society that always helps each other when trouble befalls them. They know their neighbors, whereas the English can live next-door to someone for years and never know them. The Amish take care of their elderly; they don't need or want anything from the government such as Social Security or food stamps or welfare or any other government hand out. The Amish have never lost a member of their faith to wars, because the Amish don't believe in fighting wars; they won't defend this country, period. As a whole, they are classified by the Federal Government as conscientious objectors.

Amish schools go to the eighth grade. There is usually one teacher, but sometimes two if there are over 25 children. Amish children do not know how to speak English until they go to school because Pennsylvania Dutch is the common language among the Amish. Pennsylvania Dutch is a dialect of German, Dutch, and English mixed. The courses of study in school are Arithmetic, English, Writing, Vocabulary, Reading, Spelling and Social Studies and on some occasions Science. Amish schools are graded on a common scale. There can be no comparison between Amish schools and English schools because of scale differences. Amish school has 15-25 students, where English schools can have from 300 to 2500 depending on the area.

Discipline in Amish schools is far more strict because Amish believe in corporal punishment. They have no laws to contend with; therefore a teacher may whip a child. Then when the child gets home, he or she will get another whipping, even more serious.

A sheriff's deputy in a Northern Indiana county said that of all the drug problems in his area, Amish young people were often in the middle. He also said that certain bishops of the Amish had to come bail their children out of jail and take them home.

A local motel in Shipshewana, Indiana has had several rooms totally trashed when rented by young Amish in order to have parties, drink beer, smoke pot, and whatever else takes place when young men and women get together. The manager of this motel said that this occurs quite often in the spring and fall. He smiles and says, "Amish young people ain't no different than anyone else." The report could go on and on in different areas around the country; Iowa, Indiana, Illinois, Ohio, and Pennsylvania. But because the Amish represent a large number of people in these areas and the tourist trade depends on people coming to see the Amish, most of these infractions of the law are washed away by the local authorities because the Amish bishops promise to handle the punishment themselves.

Recently in Lancaster County, Pennsylvania, two Amish men, members of the Old Order Amish community, were arrested for buying and distributing cocaine and other drugs. One of the men has claimed that he has been using drugs for the last five years. Amish leaders are always warning their young people about the English and their evil ways, but what about the evil in the midst of the Amish? Will Amish bishops and their other leaders again beg for leniency for these misguided poor souls who did not know what they were doing, while pointing the finger at the English in order to blame everyone but the guilty ones? What about letting the law deal with these men, Amish or English, and let the hammer fall on the guilty? If these men stepped outside the boundaries of the church and broke the law, then they should pay the price just like everyone else.

In certain Amish communities in Northern Indiana, more and more Amish men are working in English factories building mobile homes. Therefore, these men do receive tax refund checks, unemployment checks, and when they retire they do receive Social Security checks. Not all Amish do, but some do.

Now as far as the Amish being conscientious objectors, that is all well and good, if they really believe in their faith, but let's look at what happened at the beginning of the Desert Storm War. An Amish bishop told me himself, that more young men of the Amish faith joined the church throughout the country, than at any other time in the history of the Old Order Amish when the United States entered into war with Iraq. They sold their cars, changed their clothes, threw away their radios, kissed their English girlfriends goodbye, and ran home to the Amish just as fast as they could because they believed that the Government would enact the draft and they would have to go to war and fight. When I asked the bishop how he felt, he replied, "Ashamed, but still they did come back, and that is all that matters."

By the look on his face, I felt he knew, as I did, that the ones who joined the church did not do it for the right reason. Therefore it is a lie, these young Amish people were actually hiding behind the Amish faith, and these young men will someday rule the church.

I am not saying that we as a nation, are any better than any one else. At least we admit that we have problems. We have laws that are there to protect people or punish those that break the law. I realize that we are not perfect, and I am sure there's a lot we can do to make things better, but for heaven's sake, we can pick up a phone and call for help. From the time a person is born into the Old Order Amish, they are taught to avoid the English because it could lead them down the path of destruction, and if they leave the Amish and go into the English world should they happen to die by whatever means, it will mean damnation. That person will go to hell with no chance of redemption simply because they are outside the Amish church.

That's a powerful tool the Amish leaders have. If someone

steps out of line or stumbles a little, the Amish bishop or ministers or even the deacon will threaten the sinner with the ban, and the person jumps back in line. Fear, fear of going to hell, fear of being shunned by their family, fear of being alone. But no matter how hard the Amish try there are always those that will find a way and leave the Amish.

The stories that you have read, are of some of those people, the ones that won't accept things as they are. They choose to worship as they believe or maybe discovered the truth in the Bible and left to find more answers. They are those that, even though afraid, left in the middle of the night because in their hearts they knew, knew what they had to do. They had to leave, and go wherever life took them. Their stories are stories of courage, determination, and perseverance. I am proud that I have met these people, and I am sure that the Almighty will be there for them as He is for everyone. Salvation is a gift from God, a gift that no man can take away from another simply because he chooses to worship in a different way, dress more modern, take a bath in the house with running water piped in, turn on electrical lights, make a phone call from his or her house, or get in his car and drive to the movie or to the market or wherever he wants to go.

If you are born Amish, you must die Amish. This is what the people of the Amish faith believe. There can be no other way, only the Amish way. What the Amish forgot is, the nature of things, meaning that people will not be held back, they will reach out and go beyond the limits of the boundaries that have been established. People will seek the truth no matter the consequences, and reach for their dreams. The Amish obviously have forgotten their past. Menno Simons and the Anabaptists left the Holy Roman Catholic Church even under penalty of death to pursue their dreams. Jacob Ammon, spiritual leader and founder of the Amish faith, left the Mennonites even under the threat of the ban and being excommunicated by the Mennonite Church. Obviously Menno or Jacob did not worry too much about the consequences of their actions. They did what they had to do to reach for their dreams and go beyond the limits of other men. Did the Amish not leave Europe and come to America seeking freedom from persecution to worship as they believed, freedom to grow, and freedom to nurture their young as they chose? They wanted the freedom to choose, but today they deny this freedom to their followers. If one

chooses a different path, then the Amish ban, shun, and excommunicate with a vengeance just as they did over three hundred years ago.
The Amish obviously have forgotten their past. If you do not remember the past then you are doomed to repeat it. It seems the more we
change things, the more things stay the same.

Bibliography

Hostetler, John A. *Amish Society*. Baltimore: The Johns Hopkins University Press, 1993.

Kraybill, Donald B. *The Riddle of Amish Culture*. Baltimore: The Johns Hopkins University Press, 1991.

Langin, Bernd G. *Plain and Amish: An Alternative to Modern Pessimism*. Scottdale, Pennsylvania: Herald Press, 1994.

Nolt, Steven M. *A History of the Amish*. Intercourse, Pennsylvania: Good Books, 1992